Praise for Follow the Medicine

"*Profound and Life Changing. This book will help you feel strong and empowered as you move forward in life.*"
~ Cami Walker,
New York Times Best Selling Author of *29 Gifts, How Monthly Giving Can Change Your Life*, and Creator of the 29gifts.org Movement

"Follow the Medicine *is an awakening into new ways of being, eyes wide open accessing the full potential of who you are, if that's what your seeking read this book!*"

~ Bruce Margolin, ESQ
Attorney and Cannabis Legalization Attorney

"*In her book,* Follow The Medicine, Awakening Self Empowerment, *Scarlet Ravin did an excellent job of integrating many perennial wisdoms regarding the power of mental focus, with her own life-experience anchoring these ancient truths in everyday reality. I highly recommend this book to anyone seeking to maximize their highest potential while manifesting their own life purpose.*"
~ Joseph Cavanaugh, MS, MFT
Author of *Who Am I Really, How Our Wounds Can Lead to Healing*

"*Each session with Scarlet brings awareness to emerging aspects of myself. Supported by her insight and genuine care, I carry forward a sense of empowerment to embrace the life I want to create*".

~ Karen Kopacz,
Brand Strategist & Designer

Permission should be addressed in writing to Scarlet Ravin:
PO Box 1715, Forestville CA 95436

Cover Design, Killer Covers
http://killercovers.com

Editor, Lex Maritta
lexmaritta@gmail.com

Layout, Anne Karklins
annekarklins@gmail.com

First Edition, 2017

ISBN-13: 978-1-988071-70-1
ISBN-10: 1988071704

Follow

the
Medicine

AWAKENING SELF EMPOWERMENT

Scarlet Ravin

Dedicated to *all the learners out there seeking to awaken something greater within themselves. For Escotties, son of Escotties, for always being there for me no matter what. For my parents who always reminded me that I was limitless, incredible, and made of pure magic. For my brother who became a great rock for me when my ground was shaking. For all my friends who have inspired me along this path. I will forever hold gratitude for you deep in my heart for the support, love, and devotion you gave me throughout this process.*

*"If you do what you've always done,
you'll get what you've always gotten."*

~ Tony Robbins

Contents

"Never give up on a dream just because of the time it will take to accomplish it. The time will pass anyway."

~ Earl Nightingale

Foreword

The Deep Truth

You will find a lot of books in the so-called "Self Help" industry titled with "The only 3 steps to…." "The Super-Success Crating 7 Behaviours…." and "The Secret to…". The simple truth is, those books mostly give you an idea of how to rearrange the surface, and very few authors discovered on a deep-level of truth, what they are writing about. In my book "Better The Whole World Against Me Than My Soul," I shared my journey from "wow he's made it! He's a tax lawyer and financial consultant" to a really free and naturally happy person that enjoys life on all levels. Because of my sometimes very tough experiences, I can feel if an author is writing from merely their intellect and trying to sell their 200 pages, or if they write from their heart and personal experience.

The entire universe is frequency, and in-FORMation. This is how our thoughts can become things. To really heal and transform our lives and society, we all need to dig deep in ourselves and uncover our axioms that we build our stories and paradigms upon. Scarlet has walked a deep journey inwards, and been through a lot of processes to find the core beliefs in herself. The core beliefs that dictate our life, are so concealed deep in our subconscious that we are not aware of them.

Because of this, our search for health and fulfilling wealth will fail when we only look for the solutions on the outside. Because of our habitual way of thinking, it is a sometimes painful process.

The topics of personal transformation, healing, and purpose that Scarlet dives into are eternally important. We are entering into a new phase of human evolution, whereby individuals question the status-quo. Where people seek to live their lives balancing this thing called life, and not struggling against it. Living from the inside out is what all happy and wise people recommend.

And how to do it?

Scarlet will show you in this useful guide how to find your axioms that run your life, and how to reframe your hindering beliefs into strong and supporting ones, so that you can live in the flow with natural health and wealth. Nature is so good to us when we dare to live our True Self!

Please don't just read this book. Apply and live it, and unblock your True Self. If you are an Apple, just be the best Apple you can be. Don't try to be anything else.

To create synergy and synchronicity purposeful living, seek out for other individuals who want and understand the same. Take a look at the Winspiration Community (www.winspiration.global) and on the 7th of May celebrate then, with us and millions of "true fruits" around the globe. Your true essence, your purpose, your potential.

Get all your energy 100% back to you and use it for yourself, to live your true essence. This is the best way to serve the world. Only authentic true selves dare to live in a win-win society.

So turn the page and read Scarlet's book carefully, don't rush through it. Trust your gut, and feel what is good for you within these pages and start living, truly living.

Scarlet's shared wisdom will encourage not only your life. You will then also touch people, friends and family with your new happy, healthy way of living.

Be Blessed, and Happy Living!
The Best is yet to Come.

Wolfgang G. Sonnenburg

WOLFGANG SONNENBURG
winning for life

Author of "Basic Millionaire Spirit",
Founder of Winspiration Day.
www.wolfgangsonnenburg.com

Introduction

I was born into this world to create a new version of existence, and that is my very intention for writing this book. I have not always felt this way, for I perceived most of my life to be a struggle. A struggle to fit in, a struggle to feel healthy, and a struggle to know what the heck is happening on this planet. This is not a book on how to think positive, it is a book on how to train your mind to see the positive in any situation. If you can do this, you can become fully empowered, no matter how much shit life throws at you. Life will throw you curve balls, and while we do have a part in creating our own reality with our mind, we do get tested and challenged by life with circumstances completely out of our control. This is where mind training becomes crucial to succeeding. Life will never throw at you more than you can handle, and if you can see everything as an opportunity, then nothing can stop you. If you can see everything as happening for you, and not to you, then you'll be unstoppable.

While you read this book, allow it to set the groundwork for an awakening to new states of awareness, new ways of seeing the world, with the intention to allow you to remember that you're already a whole, complete, successful beautiful being. That you are not broken, you are not useless, and you most certainty are not incapable of anything you choose to set your mind to. You have more power inside of your heart than you even realize. May this book awaken your knowing to that power, then create the direction for you to channel that power, to create the life you want to live.

I can remember the very first time another kid was mean to me. You see, I used to get made fun of quite a lot for being "different." I was having an incredible session of make-believe, which was my favorite thing to do. My mind was always rich with stories, and bringing those stories to life was a taste of what God, (higher power, or whatever you feel called to reference) must feel like. It's very fulfilling to say the least. On the playground, first grade, I was pretending I was a horse. I was going to win the blue ribbon. And the entire world, which formed the crowd watching my performance, was going to stand up and cheer me on as I cleared the last fence! The pressure was building as I galloped around on my four legs, jumping bushes and seeing them as six-foot oxers. Then I landed my last fence, and hurray! The crowd rose and went wild as I brought my horse back to a trot, and began to walk towards the judge to claim my blue ribbon!

What an excitement, as I had never jumped that course before and there I was, getting a championship! Turns out, if you're five years old, running around on all four legs, jumping bushes and other imaginary fences in front of a recess class, you're going to get a mouthful of insults. And insults I got. They called me a freak, and ridiculed me for the rest of that school year. Deep inside I can remember thinking, *they must not have seen how high those fences were that I was jumping, because if they had, they would have known what an incredible accomplishment this was.*

This, my dear friends, was just the beginning of my walk through this world, and the ridicule didn't end in elementary school. Eventually I just stopped talking and began to talk to my pony, who was a real pony. My trainer at the time sparked some concern, as she had never heard my voice. She spoke to my mother about it and my mother replied with, "she won't stop talking at home!" But out in the thick of the outside world, it was my inner world that fueled me, my imagination. I was constantly jumping street signs and bushes, as I rode my horse in my mind alongside the school bus as I was being carted off to school. That imaginary horse could jump eight feet! I am not kidding!

When it came to socializing with other kids, most of them found me quite strange. I had a reputation as a freak, which can be a hard one to shake. As my friend group grew smaller and smaller, my inner world grew larger and larger until I found myself with a horse as a best friend, and a strong pull to want to leave this cruel world.

Back then, I didn't know why we were all alive, why we were all walking on this planet doing what we do. I knew in my heart that if we weren't going to just love and support one another, then I didn't want to stick around. I struggled, with massive amounts of inner pain, and a huge sense of confusion.

Alongside my keen imagination, I was also blessed with an extremely sensitive empathic system, where I could feel all that was going on around me. People didn't even have to open their mouths, and I could feel what they felt. When they spoke to me, I knew if they were lying or telling the truth, and oh my how people lie. I would say more than half of the time adults lie to children, and think they are clueless. I knew. I knew every time, which only added to my confusion as to why I was here. And what was with all these people, who seemed to live in an entirely different way than I felt comfortable living.

I got into drugs in high school to numb myself to the massive amount of things I felt, not just from other people, but pains from the planet, the animals, and the frustration of the teachers before me. It was overwhelming, and I had no tools to deal with my inner self, so I checked out.

After a substantial amount of years checked out, hiding from my authentic self as I never felt this world was made for me, I hit my rock bottom of frustration and said no more. I began to soul search. I travelled across the USA more than once, as well as many foreign countries, seeking answers to these soul driven questions I had carried with me since my youth. I realized I had a lot of healing to do. I found answers, then moved on to my next questions and continued this journey for over fifteen years.

Filled to the brim with healing arts certifications, and a bundle of gifted knowledge, still most days felt like an inner struggle. Until, I went to a Bob Proctor seminar in Los Angeles and experienced his awareness training. It was the last key that allowed all the other information to fall into place.

From that moment on, my world was mine. I knew for the first time why I never fit in, and why I never looked, or acted like the rest of the world. I was never meant to. I was put here to create a new world for us all to enjoy. This book is the offering of my introduction into how one can carry themselves in this new world, where one has, and knows they have the ability to create the life they want. Where they know how to manage their inner emotions, and bring about a life with love, health, and abundance in every sense of the word.

A world where you can see yourself, as I see you. A perfectly imperfect person filled to the top with love, delight, drive, creativity, and a unique offering that you have to give to this world. You are here. And inside of you is a gift that we all want and need. I set the intention to share this book with you, hoping it activates an empowerment within yourself to love yourself, see yourself as God's highest creation, see yourself in charge of your own health and wellness. You can have everything you want in this life. You can take charge of your thoughts and bring to you, your deepest hearts desire. If your health is poor, or you're struggling to heal your body, this book can walk you through the very steps that will bring you vibrant health, and overall wellness. If you want to bring more abundance in the form of money into your life, this book will activate the knowing inside of yourself, of how to do just this. If you want better love relationships, or you want to attract that perfect partner, this book will be offering the insight to show you just how to do this.

I may use the word God in this book, and I use it to reference of the higher power of this world. You may refer to this as universal consciousness, higher self, spirit, earth, and anything else you wish to reference. For me, the word God used to have such a heavy weight to it, as I rejected all of the God, prayer, religious notions of this world. One of the greatest shifts I have had in this life, is allowing my triggers to fade, and to train myself to see through to what's more important, which is communication and raising the awareness of this world. So if you're not into the word God, I totally get it. Just replace it when I use it, with something that feels more soothing to your soul.

You are God's highest form of creation, you're here to walk this planet, and create the world you want to live in. If you feel like you don't fit in, then good! Create a new world that resonates with you. That is why you're here! The masses may walk together, asleep. And that's okay, they will wake up as more and more of us wake up around them, for we are all made of energy and therefore offer up a resonance to all of those traveling around us. You want to help the world? Help yourself first, and the world will follow.

This book is not meant to be read once, for many of us have been programmed for years and years, and those programs may be resting deep in our subconscious minds. Our goal here is to reprogram the subconscious mind with new information, so that everything I just spoke about that is available to you in this life is a knowing, and not just an idea. In order for us to make this a knowing, we must repeat, dedicate time, and follow through with applying new teachings. This is an offering up of new perspectives for you to examine. And if you can integrate these viewpoints through positive, inspired eyes when life gets tough, because it will get tough, you'll come out stronger. When life is easy and flowing perfectly, you'll keep your mind focused on the positive in order to enhance, and grow that wealth of positivity.

If this sounds like work, then ask yourself this. Are you happy? Are there things in your life you would like to change? Are there health issues you want to heal? Are those yearnings worth answering? Is this life worth it to you? Yes? Then join me on an adventure to walking through this new world that we can create together. A world where we love all of those around us, we cherish the time we get with our family, we support, nurture, and honor EVERY being on this planet. No matter how big or how small.

Let's activate a soft kindness within ourselves that serves everyone around us like we are serving God. And when you look in the mirror, my goal is to have you know without a doubt, that you are amazing, you are incredible, and you are a blessing to this world. We need you. We need your gift, for you are the only one that has it, and it's imperative to me that you start standing up for the empowerment of yourself. Know you're creating your own life, take responsibility, and then change it.

I also want to state, that wherever you are on your journey right now is perfect, and if some of these suggestions seem far out of reach, like they would have felt for me 15 years ago, then read this book. Plant some seeds in your subconscious mind, and do the very best you can every day. Wherever you are is perfect, and the heights you can reach in this life are endless. My prayer is that these words help to uplift you into seeing yourself as I see you, which is perfect. A soul working on raising one's awareness, until they themselves know that they are incredible just the way they are, and inspired just as they are. They merely have to awaken to it.

Another brick for the building of your awareness house, is this: some of us, including myself, have been through some heavy shit in our lives. Trauma, as well as other physical ailments that we didn't ask for. These circumstances must be dealt with, and cleansed. There is no amount of positive thinking that can "wish" away anything with a cover-up like mind set. One must cleanse the physical body of trauma, and this can be done through somatic psychology, body work, and gestalt therapy to just mention a few techniques. Once there is a balance gained in the body, then you'll have the power to keenly train your mind to create your own reality, while also utilizing the trained focus of your mind to direct your thoughts towards the positive, in any given challenging moment in your life. Life is practice, and the best moments of growth are not resting in the happy, easy-breezy moments, but resting in the challenges, and the times when we are tested.

I suggest that you underline or highlight the passages that call to you, then when you read the book a second and third time, you'll have a gauge to see how your awareness is shifting. You'll begin to see yourself change in such a short time, and this reward will be the greatest feeling for your soul.

There will be stories referenced in this book. They are real stories from real life circumstances, which I have changed the names of the people mentioned to keep their privacy intact, as this book reaches the hands of millions of people.

PART I

Blackbird

Blackbird singing in the dead of night
Take these broken wings and learn to fly
All your life
You were only waiting for this moment to arise.

Blackbird singing in the dead of night
Take these sunken eyes and learn to see
All your life
You were only waiting for this moment to be free.

Blackbird fly, blackbird fly
Into the light of the dark black night.
Blackbird fly, blackbird fly
Into the light of the dark black night.

Blackbird singing in the dead of night
Take these broken wings and learn to fly
All your life

You were only waiting for this moment to arise
You were only waiting for this moment to arise
You were only waiting for this moment to arise

"The Beatles"

CHAPTER ONE:

How the Medicinal Seeds Sprouted, the Birth of Awareness

"Your time is limited, so don't waste it living someone else's life. Don't be trapped by dogma, which is living with the results of other people's thinking. Don't let the noise of other's opinions drown out your own inner voice. And most important, have the courage to follow your heart and intuition. They somehow already know what you truly want to become. Everything else is secondary."

~ Steve Jobs

Many dear ones walking the planet are aching for an inner change, aching for some peace of mind. They look outwards for teachers to show them the way to inner happiness, but how does this seeking come to pass? How do we drive ourselves from mere seekers, to actually achieving what it is we strive for when it comes to our overall life, happiness and health?

There is an idea one coined as "the dark night of the soul," where one being has hard time after hard time. It can be a representation of their life circumstances, or their physical health. This dark night is their dwelling in their unhappiness for too long, or one has been sick in health for too long and this misfortune has then turned into a desire for change. This unhappiness, this negative feeling, this pain has then transferred into our motivation to seek answers. This IS the seed of drive, this IS the seed that is then planted inside our minds that will then carry us to new heights within our life if we so choose to follow and nurture this new goal, happiness.

Before we go too deep, let's take a moment to honor what we choose to perceive as misfortunes in our health and life. For most of the time, it is one in the same. We have been living our lives day in and day out, doing what it is we always do, with a slight edge of unhappiness always lurking around the next corner. Feeling kind of content, but never really satisfied. Then one day we are sick, we have been diagnosed with a disease, and we feel we have been cursed in our lives once again. That way of looking at this situation is a choice of mere perception. It is a choice a being can take and be dragged down by, what could be perceived as a gift, or be lifted into a new state of drive and desire. By seeing what has come into their lives as a gift, a new direction, a new seed planted leading that person to a new life! This is very exciting news indeed...

The sheer power of our perception will then activate the feelings in our body, and where does perception come from? Our thoughts, the way we choose to think, and the meaning we place on what we think is the drive of our perception. If one has a negative attitude, they then have a tendency of perceiving things around them from that perceptual lens. However, if one chooses to take a positive attitude towards life, then they tend to look through their eyes with a positive realm over everything they perceive.

I am not suggesting that getting the diagnoses of a disease is something to rejoice in, I know this is a rough path and one with many intense emotions tied in, but what I am saying is that we can see any diagnoses of our health as a gift, and walk down a healing path with eyes of curiosity and watch for the gifts that this new situation has presented to our lives. If we are going to have to go through something intense and disruptive in our lives, we may as well do this with grace and the KNOWING that there IS a take away in EVERY situation. And every situation has the opportunity to be perceived as a blessing, or a downfall. That is the power within you, the power to CHOOSE how you see things.

For the moments that pass in your life everyday, how many of them do you revel in? How many of them do you stop to just say to yourself, "wow, this world really is magic!" This is a practice I am asking you to undertake, as once the imagination is fully activated, and the eyes of a child are brought back into your life, your life will change. This strength you can cultivate can carry you through what you would have once perceived as the darkest of times.

I would love to lay the stage, as why we are here as beings, in bodies having lives on this planet. Once again, if we don't have the same definition of what we are speaking about, then we are bound to miss one another's visions, but I offer you this perspective of why our souls are here on this planet at this time. We are born into bodies, and our souls are here to evolve into higher states of awareness by the practice of self-realization that we are already whole unto ourselves. We already have all the magic and wisdom within ourselves, all we have to do is know that as a fact. There are certain situations that may present themselves to us during this earth-walk that will show us that we are already a perfect, beautiful, wise soul. Typically our greatest realization of strength is when we have to walk through the toughest moments in life.

Once we have this level of self-awareness, we can then reach out to others around us and help them to realize their own inner-beauty, their own inner-wisdom and their own control over the life they desire. We are here to serve others, here to realize our self as a whole divine being, and here to create whatever it is our soul is aching to create. For that is our true gift as humans. To walk this walk, without touching into our gift, is to walk this life saying, "I don't want the magic you bestowed on me God, I would rather suffer and that's my choice." And suffer you shall, if you ignore the burn in your heart of whatever it is you came here to create.

Here is a recap:

1. We are here to evolve and awaken to our own knowingness that we are whole unto ourselves, and have within us everything we need to create the life, vitality, and health we desire.

2. Once awakened, we then have the chance to serve others, and lift them into the knowing of what we have learned within ourselves.

3. We then share the greatest gift we have been given, our own unique signature to the rest of the world so they may watch the world evolve and grow through the beautiful gifts we have all been given.

The stage is set and now that we are on the same page, I move back to the story of the mundane life lived by an individual walking through life asleep, year after year. This person, we will call her Grace, she craves to love herself. She craves to have the confidence to share her life's dream, which is to travel the world and help poverty-stricken children have good lives. In fact, she has been dreaming of this dream since she was a child and her family lived in poverty. She felt the dark pain of not having enough, and made an inner vow to herself to help other children not feel what she had to feel. She promised to herself secretly that she would make enough money to fly around the world, and save children from what she went through. She felt this vision tug at the very strings of her soul.

Grace grew older. She graduated college, then was stuck paying student loans. So she took the first job she could find, worked this job day in, day out and soon that childhood vision of helping other poverty-stricken children went so far out the window, she actually believed this idea to be crazy. How was she to ever succeed in saving children, if she was having a hard time paying her student loans and paying her rent? How was she going to break out of this prison that she created for herself? Yes, I said it. She created this prison for herself.

Grace walks through life with no self confidence, she doesn't see herself with the knowing that she is God's greatest creation. That she has within her being all the wisdom, magic, drive, confidence, and beauty that she needs to accomplish any goal she may desire. However, Grace doesn't seem to know that. Why is that?

Without struggle we can not grow, without problems to work out, we do not develop. So Grace has been given a life lesson, and instead of striving to seek for answers to awaken herself to what she is innately, she blames the external world, and even herself for her struggle. This repeats the cycle of lack of self-confidence and self-betrayal of her life dreams, which continues to drive the nail of disappointment through her heart.

One day Grace feels a pain in her side, and since she has been at the same job for 10 years, she has obtained great health insurance. So she goes to the doctor to find out she has cancer. The cancer is in her kidney, and they must operate immediately. For an instant after the diagnoses, Grace feels her whole life flash before her eyes. This is the gift. She is getting a life review before her life has ended. She is getting a swift kick in the pants to seek inner self-awareness before it's too late. She then has another decision to make, she can view this as yet another curse and lay down and die, or she can stand up and fight and reclaim her life!

Grace undergoes the surgery. They remove the cancer-filled kidney, then start her on chemotherapy. As she lay in the chair recovering, while receiving the poison to kill the cancer, she begins to ponder fully for the first time in her life. Because she now has the perspective of how precious life is, and how it can dissipate in just one instance. She watches her life story in her head, and sees how she once had dreams, but allowed them to lay dormant within her as she allowed fear to guide her. She allowed worry to pull her. She sees how one decision she made after another took her to the place she is at now, and she begins to thank the cancer.

She begins to express a profound gratitude for the perspective that cancer has given her, and she begins to feel that drive from childhood regain its strength within her. Her body feeling lifeless and sick from her treatment, didn't stop the inner drive that began to grow. She started to plan her course through Africa, and which towns she was going to visit as she got well enough to travel. She began to picture the faces of the children she would hold and save, and feel their delight as they were given health care and nutrient-rich food. She began to awaken to all of life's possibilities that were once just a forgotten idea left in childhood.

As her treatment wrapped up, Grace walked into her new life, cancer free and ready to take charge of following her dreams! She was once asleep, once walking through life numbed to what she could become, and what she had to offer to this planet. Now her walk shakes the earth as she strives to make a difference, and realized it was inside of her being all along.

Thank God cancer came into her life to shake her up and awaken her to her true potential.

This story is a chosen perspective, one in which an external circumstance forced Grace to either die, or take charge of her life. It may seem like an extreme example, but it shows what many of us do every day, we walk through life with negative inner self-talk, ruining our very own self confidence, which we NEED in order to be able to make anything happen. Then we ride life like it's happening to us, rather than walking through life making it what we wish. This is our choice to make, and our life to create, and everything you need is already inside of you. You just need to plant the seed of what it is you desire, and water that seed with all your might.

Awareness has the opportunity of coming in many different forms. Many of us are just drawn to spirit. We see that inside of spiritual practices lays our own awakening, so we are drawn to things like yoga, meditation, people like Tony Robbins and Bob Proctor, and we see how other beings have created the life they want to live through realizing how to cultivate their minds. It does all come back to the mind.

What is it you are thinking to yourself every day? How do you see yourself, and how do you feel about what you are giving back to this world? Are you walking your walk, or are you just talking about things you want to do without taking action?

These questions are just the beginning for you to start to see how you have designed the very reality you live in. This has a direct link to your body's health and wellness, as well as a direct link as to how you'll be able to heal what has come into your life. Are you experiencing a health wake up call like Grace? Are you seeing this wake-up call as a gift, or a hindrance that's stopping you from carrying out your mundane life?

These questions have done something to your system, and what have they done you may ask? They are birthing awareness inside of your being as we speak. Awareness starts with a question... the seeking of that very answer is the evolution of awareness. It is all very simple, and all very elementary. And since everything is already inside of your being, it isn't something you even have to obtain externally, it is something you merely have to awaken inside of yourself. This awakening, this knowing, comes from asking questions. And if you don't have the answer, you then make a choice to seek that very answer with every spark of your being, for that seeking will lead you to the life and health you desire for yourself.

Awareness questions:

1. How do I see myself?

2. Is my lens of perception positive or negative?

3. Do I have self-confidence?

4. Do I believe in myself?

5. What is my greatest gift to the world in this lifetime? (it does not have to be just one thing, however, pick one and go for one with an unstoppable drive, then move forward with your other gifts as to keep the energy focused.)

6. Do you watch your thoughts?

7. Do you ever think or just allow your mind to wander day in and day out?

These questions I lay before you, are seeds you can plant into your awareness that will begin to awaken your consciousness, and allow you to begin to take note of where you are in space and time. Once you have noted your location, you can then change course and aim your arrival, right at the very dream you awoke with at birth. It's your greatest gift, it lays inside of your being, and you are the only one on this planet with the gift you have. The way you give this gift to the world will be unique, as there is literally only one of you. Only one person in the world that can do what you can do the way you can do it, and what part of you really wants to keep that from the rest of us? We want, need, and will glow brighter if you choose to share your gift. As a group of beings on this planet, we are all connected, for everything is energy and everything can feel what is around it. If you cultivate yourself, if you choose to raise your awareness, you are then raising the vibration of the entire planet.

That old attitude of *I am so small, what is my impact going to have* is worn out, it's dead. And a new world lays before us as we step into a beautiful sense of awakening. WAKE UP! We do need you! We need the gift you were given, and we request for you to shine that gift upon us. That is your life mission. By shining through that very gift, you will be showing others who are asleep how to awaken, you will be showing others how easy it can be to walk the life you are here to live. And how when you make the choice to do so, you bring so much light into this world. We will all be blinded by the love we feel for you as a spark of God's highest creation.

I say God as a universal term for the higher consciousness, you're more than welcome to change God to whatever term feels best to your heart with the higher power that governs this world, as it's all the same to me and everyone else. God is felt. Higher powers are known, and since there are no real words that can describe what it is, due to the limiting boxes that words create, let's just use the term "God" now with the intention of getting a life changing point across to other beings.

As you begin your journey into a state of being awake from your deep slumber, I say this to you, be kind to yourself. Be soft, be gentle, and hold yourself as you would hold a tiny baby that has just entered into this world, for that is what you are again now. You are a tiny baby in a world full of intensities. There is no sense in being hard on yourself, for this is not the fuel for self confidence, compassion, love, and dedication. These are the terms used to describe the alchemy of what it takes to breed self-confidence within your being.

Awaken to your current state of self-confidence with these questions:

1. Are you kind to yourself?

2. Would you say you treat yourself and nurture yourself like you would an infant?

3. Do you look in the mirror each morning and see sheer perfection and beauty looking back at you?

4. Do you dedicate time to yourself daily to show yourself that you love yourself? If no…Why not?

5. Do you wish you were something you currently are not? Why?

6. What questions do you need answers to in order to fully love and except yourself for who you are?

I am not exempt from awakening from being a sleep-walker through this life. I didn't love myself, didn't believe in myself, and had no sense of direction. I have walked through the toughest terrain in some occasions seeing the darkest parts of this world, and I made it out. It was because I was living and operating in this dark and dismal place, that I was able to cultivate the drive to leave them. The destructive path I initially chose in my life, led me to where I am now. I am grateful for all of it.

I awoke after spending years addicted to drugs. Numbing out at every chance I got, choosing to not love myself. So I put myself into jobs that dragged my self-confidence even lower. I used my body to create my income, and never once considered that my heart and mind were my true gifts, the body just happened to be the vessel. I ran myself down until one day I took so many drugs I couldn't carry on, and this was my bottom. This bottom was also my greatest gift, because I had drive. I was driving myself to death. I was driving myself into the ground, because I didn't think I was worthy to be on this planet. The greatest insight I took from this experience was that, I realized my drive was unstoppable. Whether I directed that drive into killing myself, or ruining my own life, it was drive nonetheless. And If I were to re-direct that drive into another area of my life, perhaps a positive change in my life, then that same drive would then carry me to new heights of self.

This was when my seed was planted. I was then in my early 20's and filled with more self-hatred than a will to live. I always wanted to die. I always thought this planet was not suitable for me, that I was meant to live in a place that was more kind, more gentle, and more loving. What I had yet to realize, is that I was put here to create that new world that I so strived to live in. I am here to create with my God-given abilities, a world in which we do seek love for one another, we do seek compassion for one another above all else. We support one another in self-growth, and loving ourselves infinitely. I am here to create a world in which you see how others see you, so you then see yourself with such grace and love, and that is what begins to breed. The love, the compassion, the understanding of the struggle of what it means to be human is just that, understanding.

To be able to have this understanding for others, we must cultivate this within ourselves. We must commit right here and now, to begin to love ourselves. To seek any means necessary to learn how to raise our awareness, how to love ourselves, and how to activate the gift God gave us in our hearts, to then share with the world. We are here to create a new world. And if these words resonate with your being, you know this is true. You know you were placed here to create a new world, and you know that must first begin by you having the courage and drive to first begin by cleaning up your own backyard. This is NOT the time to blame your external circumstances. This is the time you go inside. You cultivate yourself just like all the other great beings have done before you, and you begin to walk the walk your heart has been speaking to you, for perhaps decades. Now is the time.

CHAPTER TWO:

Walking Through Life Asleep

"In essence, if we want to direct our lives, we must take control of our consistent actions. It's not what we do once and while that shapes our lives, but what we do consistently."

~ Anthony Robbins

The intention of this chapter is to lay the groundwork for insight, as to how one can tune into the message coming from the body, and allow those messages to direct one on how to take care of themselves, therefore loving themselves. There are many ways to come into a state of health. By caring about what you put into your body, as well as how you see your body, will then ripple out into the rest of your life. Authenticity and congruency in self-care, does permeate out into the world... As within... so without...

As the sun shines bright, and the sky dances with the clouds, we walk through life making daily decisions that then disperse into our current reality. We may be in seventy-degree weather, living in a perfectly healthy body, plenty of money in the bank, but still not happy.... Why?

Why are there so many humans on this planet living in dire circumstances, and many others happy with nothing? Why are some living in mansions, and some living on the street?

Growing up with plenty of my own inner-concerns to weed through, I began to seek answers at a very young age. I began to question why things were the way they were. When I didn't receive an answer I felt satisfied with, I simply chose to continue digging for something with more depth and resonance. I could actually feel deep in my soul when something rang as a truth for me, and when this truth bell rang, I was able to then resonate with the answer and use that information to gain deeper awareness and insight into my life. I have to admit, I didn't know what I was doing. I was just simply following my heart. Now at the ripe age of 35 I currently have the insight to look back and see... I was following the medicine.

Before we get too deep into the medicine I found, let's first get on the same page of what medicine means. We can't really compare apples to oranges, because they are simply just different fruit. But if we both are holding apples, then we have a stage where comparison will lead to growth, rather than argument. I often found myself creating my own definitions to words as I was growing up, along with my own way of spelling. I found that when someone said a word to me that I hadn't known before, I would define it by how it made my heart feel. I would often spell it quite different as well, and I continue to live in that vibration of my own creation still, as I often find certain words limiting with their current definition.

I define medicine as this: " *The internal knowing that all answers and paths to health and wellness, already rest inside our being. And through the act of raising our awareness while empowering oneself, we have access to a medicine which is none other than the awareness that everything already rests within our own being.*"

So when grandma says to you, "honey, it's time for you to take your medicine!" She is truly saying this, "honey, you may be feeling ill right now, but if you choose to stay positive and raise your awareness, you will imprint your subconscious, and that will then resonate with your body leading you into a state of perfect health and wellness." That's what I mean by medicine. I re-define, re-create, then walk in the world I was placed here to awaken. This is my mission, and this is why I am writing this book.

As beings walk through life, some may be feeling physically ill, some may be feeling mentally ill, some emotionally ill, but most of all of them are feeling disempowered when it comes to leading themselves into a state of health and wellness. We are at a crucial time in our world where people are beginning to wake up to the fact that Western medicine has large swiss cheese sized holes in it. That doesn't mean the cheese isn't good on a sandwich when you add a little mayo and turkey, but it does mean it's not a complete one-stop-shop to perfect health.

I would love to plainly state that this book is in no way discrediting modern Western medicine, nor is it suggesting you don't use Western doctors. I am simply adding a new path on the walk to wholeness, and trust me, there are many, many paths that lead to the same destination of health, wealth and vitality! This path is mine, and I offer it to you hoping it awakens something inside of your being, that allows your awareness to rise up. Then you can awaken the ability to heal yourself and others.

As we are born into this world, we are given what I like to call a "skin suit." We fit into it most of the time, sometimes we burst right out when we expand, but nonetheless we must deal with our body, and how we view that relationship is the first step to wholeness. Taking the time to rest, nourish, and love our bodies is something that many people who are asleep, find to be a burden. They think that running through life, stacking their accomplishments up higher and higher, is their true path to happiness. It may be, but once you reach that goal if you don't have a body to enjoy your riches with, you really have nothing.

If one does not take the time to listen to the body's messages, and one doesn't get messages when one is consciously asleep, then the messages get louder and louder until they either kill us, or push us into a corner and make us change our lives. Luckily I have put my physical body through many experiments, not knowing at the time I was doing research for this book, but now my past life research will come in handy for you.

Simply put, our bodies are always talking to us. Let's put it like this so you can hear me, because many people shy away from listening to another present them with physical health ideas, but can often receive a metaphor saying the same thing.

The Story of the Great Boy and his Totem of a Destiny

There once was this great big island, off the coast of Greece. It was only inhabited by ten people, and always had been. Every time a new person was born the oldest would die, and this pattern went on for centuries. It was just how things worked on this island. Once a new person was born, they were given a tool that was to last them the rest of their days. There was also only one job on the island, and that job was to carve the largest totem pole ever created. It had been worked on for thousands of years, and continued to get more and more detailed as the years passed. One of the new humans that was born, was presented with their said totem tool on his fifth birthday. Oh, how overjoyed he was to begin his life-task of carving! He was so overjoyed that he jumped up and down, screaming with excitement, and the tool flung out of his hand and into the sand.

One of the elders came to him and said, "now dear one, you have only one tool in this life, you will never get a replacement, and your task at hand is quite huge. So please take care of your tool, keep an eye on it, and tune it up when it begins to break. It can last forever if you choose to give it the right care and attention."

The boy heard the old man and nodded, then ran over to his section of the totem and began his life's work. He was a special young boy, and his art became acclaimed. Through this acclamation he began to get full of himself, and he worked longer and longer hours, and harder than anyone else on the totem. His focus became so intense, he forgot to care for his tool, and one day the spring inside of it popped right out and became lost in the sand.

The boy now being 13 years old, went to the elder who gave him the tool, and showed him the missing spring hole. Looking up with dismay he said, "have you got any extra springs? Mine is lost forever in the sand." The elder looked at his tool. Then he looked back at the boy and responded, "now son, I told you when I gave you your tool, that you would only get one. I think it may serve you to slow down and care for the tool that will help you succeed on this island, or you may be in grave danger if you break your tool, then must sit out the rest of your life."

The boy heard the elder, but what overcame what he heard? His inner ego of course! So he ran back to the totem with even more determination, and carved twice as hard as before, because now he had to create the inner leverage that the spring did naturally. The over-compensation he began to play with, began to drain him slowly. He worked just as long as the others on the island, but was getting tired at a much quicker pace now that he had to overcompensate. Due to his tiredness from having to use extra work, he tripped on a rock on his way home from work and fell with his tool in his hand. As he slammed into the sand, the tool bumped up against a hard rock and split into two pieces. Now he was really screwed.

He arrived at the totem the next day with his head hung low, and his heart heavy. He gazed up at the elder saying nothing, just holding up his tool, which rested in two separate pieces. The elder gazed at the tool and said, "this is grave indeed my son. It seems you have not yet heeded my wisdom on going slow to go further in this life. You chose to charge ahead with gusto, and now you have no working tools to do the work you were placed on this earth to do. I am sorry, but we must send you off into the woods to figure out another way to carve your part of the totem. It's the only way."

The young boy had never known this to have happened, for he had only been the on the island since birth, which was thirteen years. He was grief stricken, and his heart pounded with fear, as he left all that he knew and walked off into the woods to sit with what he had done, and to make peace with the loss he created for himself.

He sat. He pondered and gazed up at the sky, begging for help. He placed his hands on the earth, and begged the earth to hold him. He cried and cried and cried, and after a week of despair he realized, that he was the one who broke his tool. Maybe he could be the one to fix it as well, so he would be able to finish his life's mission! This was a great drive for him. As he ran back to the elder who sent him away, out of breathe he shouted, "I know what I must do! I know what I must do!"

The elder turned around in his slow, turtle-like fashion, and looked down at the excited boy. He said, "yes my son? What is the plan?"

The young boy spoke, still trying to catch his breathe as he said, "I was the one who broke my tool because I was too much in a hurry, and I wasn't present. But I realized if I use one half of my tool, I can still make marks, I won't be able to do the whole task I was meant to do, but I can carve, then leave the fine detail to someone who has a tool that works. I can do that, can't I?"

The elder gazed at the young boy, smiled, and said "you can do that dear one. Using just half of your tool will indeed make your job twice as hard as it could have been, but nonetheless I think you can still make an impact and help the tribe with their project. I hope you have learned your lesson on moving slower to go further, and listening to the precious needs of the tool that is going to help you fulfill our destiny."

The boy nodded and walked back to the totem, began to carve out each stroke with a solid present gaze, now knowing how precious this small metal tool really was to him and his life.

This story is my way of showing you how precious your physical body is to your unlimited success you have access too. I was once this young boy, too driven to hear the messages my body was giving me, and due to choosing to listen to my drive rather than my system, I got sick

It was a time in my life where I chose to buy a house, build a business that would support my dreams, while simultaneously running another business to support the business I was trying to start. Simply put, I was working twelve-hour days. Hustling through the day, sleeping like a rock, then waking to get up and do it all over again. My whole system was being financially driven. For I created the reality that I needed to do this in order to survive, and to have the money to pay for my house, the new business, and also pay my mortgage for the first five months until my new business started producing a supportive income. This went on for a year, and once my new business began to take off I realized I had not had a massage, or gone for a run, or made myself a meal throughout that whole process. My system was taxed. I was about to find out just how taxed I was when I let my system unwind.

I chose to see a DDC Homeopath to do a once over on my system, and while he was doing his tests to tune into my system, he concluded that my system was too toxic to even move into a deeper diagnoses. So first step: Cleanse.

He put me on supportive cleansing tinctures that were vibrational, and three days later I was covered in shingles all over my torso. If you have ever had shingles, then you will know what I am talking about when I say it's the most painful experience I have ever had in my life. I felt lightning bolts of pain run through my body as my nerve endings died. I couldn't breath most moments, and eating CBD edibles and laying on my heated bio-mat was all I could do to survive the pain. Luckily I was surrounded by herbalists who filled my cup with healing herbs, and CBD oils, so I cleansed the shingles in just nine days, and had no permanent nerve damage. But what I didn't know, was that my unwinding was just beginning.

The shingles was followed by a cold and flu, which left me bedridden for ten days, followed by my mouth filling with sores and my lips swelling. That was followed by hives covering my face and body, itching me into a state of hysteria. Once that cleared, I was trampled by my horse. Being served a hefty concussion, following that came another cold/flu that took me to bed for another two weeks. I was better for a month, then discovered a large lump on my thyroid. Having to go get an ultrasound and biopsy, the doctor drained it and deemed it a cyst, but nonetheless my body was talking loud! This process spanned over a four-month period. Ups and downs, symptoms after symptoms, and flailed in dismay as I had taken the tool God gave me. I used it haphazardly, then sat in wonder why it wasn't working for me anymore.

There is a reaction to every action we do with our health. That year I was asleep, I was asleep to the messages my body was telling me, as all I could hear was my drive to meet my goal, my drive to get a house, and own my own business. I thought going faster meant I would get somewhere quicker, but really it meant I would get the legs knocked right from under me so that my pace would slow to a more self-serving one. One that I could live with. You see, our bodies aren't talking to us because they want to own us, or slow us down, they are talking to us because they know we have a purpose here on earth. And they want to help us succeed in accomplishing our life goals. If we take advantage of our body, it will speak up and knock us down. If we take care of our body and listen, move slowly to go further, then we will succeed not only with a great deal of inner peace, but we will be able to then enjoy the fruits of our success because we will then have a healthy body to live in and enjoy the life we created.

There is something that happens to the mind when we are sick or in pain for an extended period of time. The fight to stay positive becomes real. When my system was in pain and then I continued to get sick and got a concussion, I was riddled with no energy, headaches, nausea, and constant irritability due to the fact that even my everyday jobs to keep my business running, became monster tasks. I hadn't yet created a nest egg to hire out help, so I felt pigeon holed into doing the work myself, and forcing myself to work through being sick. Which only led me to being more frustrated, and swirling with inner turmoil. I began to get mad at my body. My mind began to break down, and I began to see everything from a negative lens. It was a struggle to just be grateful, and it was a struggle to want to get out of bed. My mind was sick, and it was because I didn't have a tool to work with to live through, and complete my life's purpose. My soul was crying, my head was negative, and my body stopped working.

I was tapped out. It was a tough lesson, but one I do not take lightly as I share these stories here with you now. The body speaks to us. It tells us when to slow down, and it tells us when to speed up. It will tell us if we need to eat more greens, or if we need to eat more protein. It will tell us what oils to ingest, and what and when to order food. It will show us how much to eat, and it will be upset if we eat too fast. It is literally one of the most advanced pieces of equipment on this planet. It can tune into anything, and guide us to great successes in our life. So why do we abuse our vessel?

We are sleepwalking. We are walking through life with low states of awareness, not even knowing that we have access to such intelligence, that we can listen to our system and be guided to wealth, success and happiness. Where is our heart located? In our body.... And how important is this tool? This loving sensation that rules and drives our system, lives in our body. This guide will take us places higher than we ever felt we could go, if we just choose to listen.

Before we can even consider listening, we must first awaken. Secondly we must empower ourselves to then trust our system. The path to wholeness is available. It is simple, it is fulfilling, and it will leave you with your hands full of everything you ever wanted, if you just slow down enough to listen, and honor the vessel within which you must walk this plane.

The ability to awaken ourselves to this knowing of beginning to care for our bodies, is the beginning to honor ourselves and care for ourselves in a deep way. Slow down, take a breath, and begin to feel yourself. Tune into how you feel after eating certain foods, and see if they nurture or hinder your overall health. Begin to honor yourself, and your body will guide you through this world with the best insight available. But first we must grow trust with ourselves. If we have spent years not listening to our systems, then we will need to begin to honor and nurture this relationship.

Many different diets and ways of nurturing yourself are available in this world, and they all fit some and not others. The most important thing to remember when you're trying these new ways of eating and exercising, is to remember how it makes YOU feel. Your body is not like any other system on this planet, so having the ability to discern what works for you, and what doesn't, is the start of you activating self empowerment. Take in wisdom from other sources, but always come to your own conclusion on how it makes YOU feel.

Begin this path with compassion, and patience. If you have stacked many years of looking the other way when it comes to your health, then be kind as you re-direct yourself onto a more nurturing path. Be kind as you learn new ways of eating, and taking care of yourself. And NEVER compare yourself to other people. The second we see something working for someone else and not ourselves, is just an input of more information. It's another form of communication – until you build trust with your body, you won't have the receptors built to truly know what you need. But also knowing what doesn't work, is just as good as knowing what does work.

If we can enter into this process with a childlike curiosity, then we are surely setting ourselves up for true long lasting success. This journey will be a never-ending one, but it will also be one of the most fulfilling practice you can do with yourself. For any journey of self discovery leads you closer to loving yourself, and the more you love yourself, the more able you are to love others. And my dear ones, isn't that why we are here? To love, and nurture others? Use this motivation to boost your inner fuel of self-discovery. Hold your own hand as you walk this path of self-discovery, and always honor with deep gratitude the discoveries you do make, for this focus will grow more discoveries and more awakenings. It's the foundation to your journey, and beginning this journey with this intention, will ensure you to have a beautiful, healthy body for your soul to live in while you love, honor, and live your life to the fullest!

DISCOVERY QUESTIONS

1. Tune into how you treat yourself and your health. Are you fully tuned into what your body needs?

2. Are there more nurturing ways you can treat your body and the bodies of others?

3. Do you hear the messages your physical body sends you? Do you listen to them?

4. Is your health vibrant?

5. Are you honoring your body or using your body?

6. Are you open, driven, and willing to discover how to care for yourself?

TAKE AWAYS

1. If you slow down, listen, and tune in you'll be able to open the channels of communication that will fill you with insight, and wisdom on how to care for and nurture yourself.

2. Your body is always speaking to you, and guiding you. It's a limitless tuning fork that can take you to great heights if you honor and listen.

3. The ability you have to care for yourself and love yourself, will be the direct amount of love and nurturing you can then give to other people.

4. Begin to create trust with your body and its messages, and this trust will grow and grow until you're fully being pulled and inspired by your true path in this life.

5. Set the intention to always honor, love, and nurture yourself. For this promise will carry you to new heights of awareness.

6. Slow down and listen, you will go further in this life.

7. You only get one body to live in, if you ruin it trying to rush towards your goals, once you obtain your objective you may not have a healthy life with which to enjoy all of what you have created.

CHAPTER THREE:

Seeking Answers:
Journey to the Wisdom Keepers

*"If you can learn to be still enough,
you can answer every question you have ever had
by looking into the center of a flower."*

~ Scarlet Ravin

would like to start this chapter by outlining the fact that every single being on this planet is different. We are all driven by different inner-feelings and sensations, and we all want different things. When it comes to one's own journey into the path of awakening, and raising one's awareness, that journey will look different, feel different and have different timing from other people in your life. So set this space of knowing, while I share with you my own particular journey and some of the key aspects that led to where I am now. This is not to say your journey must look like mine in order for you to awaken. I am merely sharing with you my intimate journey, with the intention it may awaken inside of you a strong pulling sensation that you have been feeling to seek answers. And after you ask yourself the inner-questions of what it is you want to clarify, or feel better about in your life, those questions will lead you to places on this earth where you will find the wisdom to enlighten yourself. For in the end you must know, no one will ever be able to enlighten you, heal you, or evolve you. You must make a firm decision to do this on your own, and you can obtain other wisdom from other enlightened beings for guidance, but the work that comes after you obtain the wisdom is all on you...

As I stated before, I hit the bottom of my sleepwalker period in my early twenties. I am a person who is so tuned into my own feelings and body. For me, to feel an internal pull towards seeking answers for a happier life, is easy to feel. The urges are quite loud and I have never, and I mean never, had the ability to not listen. Once the pull starts, I must follow the thread. For if I don't, only pain and inner-discomfort are there for me.

Once I knew I needed help after years of drug abuse, and abusing myself by putting myself in unhealthy situations, I realized I needed answers. My mother and father had both very transformational experiences at Esalen Institute in Big Sur, CA. So when I came to them crawling for help, they sent me there. I can remember the evening I drove from downtown Denver, to Castle Rock. Crying the whole drive, feeling sorry for myself, and also feeling completely lost. My mother hugged me and comforted me, as mothers are so good at, while we scrolled through the workshop options and dates. I wanted to attend a workshop that was happening ASAP to relieve myself from my own inner-pain, as soon as humanly possible.

There was a workshop called, *How Our Wounds Can Lead To Healing* by Joseph Cavanaugh, that was starting two days later. So I booked a seat in the workshop, booked a flight to Monterey, and that was that. It was the first major decision I ever made to start walking the trail that would eventually lead me so deep inside myself, that I knew without a fraction of a doubt, I was God's highest creation. I was the master of my reality, and I am the creator of all that goes on in my world.

Being as my temperament was back then, I centered around extremes. I took the bottle of pills I had with me, as I hadn't the courage to flush them quite yet. I ended up gobbling the whole bottle of painkillers on the plane, only to land in Monterey to find the nearest bar to start chugging vodka. I had two hours of waiting until the bus arrived to drive me up to Esalen. So I waited patiently in a nearby bar, until the bartender cut me off and asked me to leave. I can't exactly recall how I was behaving, but from the swift words that sent me out the door, I am sure I was probably not holding it together very well, even if my inner perceptions were deceiving me.

The bus ride was horrible as I was trying not to throw up, and also I was not sharing in the exuberance that all the other people in the bus had, as we journeyed to this sacred place. They were laughing and talking about how happy they were, and all I could feel was pain. Inner-pain that radiated through my entire body. Everything hurt. My mind, my heart, my head, my body, and most of all, my soul. For I hadn't taken the time to listen to my soul in years, and she was so ready to be heard, that by me making the choice to ignore her, it filled me with an in-authentic dismay I was unable to shake, ever. Even when I wasn't sober. And I know some of you out there know what I am speaking about.

The workshop was based in the big house, and all of the participants gathered to sit in a circle, while Joseph spoke to us about the plans for the week and his intentions for helping us. I liked him. I thought his presence was soft, and that is what I needed to open, softness. However, I was not a talker at that point in my life. In fact, I was a hider. Which now I see, is the opposite of a talker. So, my plan was to hide, make it through the week without saying a peep, then leave and I would be healed. Certainly just being in such sacred energy would heal me, and I should not have to share anything I don't want to, and that was my intention for the week!

We were all together over eight hours a day, in a very intimate realm. Other participants were sharing before the whole group what they had been through, and the hurts they sustained, and Joseph would facilitate a way for them to reclaim themselves, and see themselves as whole. No doubt, people were transforming, and that's when I realized I was withdrawing. I had been on drugs for over a decade, and this was my first five days with no access to drugs... hence the bottle dump into my mouth on the plane. I was starting to sweat, and get a headache that felt larger than an earthquake. Then my vision kept blurring, and I felt as though throwing up was my best friend.

Joseph watched me from the corner of his eye I am sure, as he had a gift for having a watchful eye for even the slightest of details. Other guests in the workshop stayed close to my side as I got sick, and they made sure I drank water and ate. And after two days of the rough nausea, the headache subsided and it was Thursday already. With the workshop about to end the next day, I believed I had almost skated through the whole week without having to share! Until....

I walked into the Thursday afternoon session and I had a hood over my head, and my eyes glued to the ground, when Joseph stepped right in front of me and said, "are you in there?" He looked at me as I tried to escape the encounter, knowing now that I couldn't. "Is there anything you want to share with the group?" he asked me, as I kept my eyes glued to the ground. I actually don't remember what I said back, all I recall is sweat pouring from my head, my hands, and down my back, and my head beginning to swell as I tried to muster words. "I'll guide you," he said, as I walked to my seat in the room.

I won't go into the deepest of depths of what I shared, but the gist was this: When I was 18 I was in a very abusive relationship. I had just left home to live in the dorms at Fort Lewis College in Durango. I was a very free spirit, and a very crazy young woman, to say the least. I was daring, and hard to catch. One day I caught the eye of a young man at the school, and he set out to make me his girlfriend. I resisted in my natural manner, and he pursued. Until one day, his romancing and gestures captured my heart, and we became boyfriend and girlfriend. At first I really enjoyed myself, but slowly and slowly, he became more and more controlling, shutting me off from my friends that were men. Then, slowly, my friends that were women as well. He began by just grabbing my arm, but eventually became abusive verbally, and physically.

He was irrational and very scary to me. He would break into my dorm at night when I would try to leave him, and trash my things. And the words he used to cut me down began to puncture my heart, until I believed them as well. After eights months of this, and many visits from the local police department, I was nothing more then a skin suit. My soul had left my body, and I had no training on how to deal with this abuse, or how to get out of it. So I made a plan in my head. At the end of the last semester, I would change my cell number, move towns and move schools, not tell anyone where I was going, and then I would be free from him ever being able to find me.

I carried out my plan very beautifully, but I never, and I mean never, spoke about what he had done to me. I went through my life after that point literally pretending nothing happened, and drugs were the only thing that helped me maintain this façade. But as we all know, that's not a walk one can maintain. And this break down I had before I went to Esalen was the building up of that event, along with other things I had chosen to interpret as misfortunes from my childhood.

For the first time, I stood before twenty people I didn't know. And with the help of Joseph, I got through the story while I cried and cried... I felt shame, and I felt weak. I also felt everyone there was going to look at me like I was a weak, little useless thing, but they didn't. They all had tears in their eyes. They all were exuding love for me at a rapid rate, and they all just wanted to hold me. I had never even considered this being a response. I was shaming myself so much and hating myself, that love was never even a consideration.

Needless to say, I felt like the weight of the world had been lifted from my shoulders, and for the first time since I could even remember, I was free! I was so light, so exuberant, and so fulfilled! I no longer even wanted to touch drugs, as for the first time I realized how much fun life could be! I had no idea! I then associated taking drugs with negative weight, and I associated being sober with clarity and love. And from that instant on, I never had the urge to even take drugs, for I saw them as the hindrance that stood in front of my heart to receive, and give authentic love! I was absolved, and this workshop was my first taste of wisdom I was to receive on my journey.

TAKE AWAY:

1. The pain became too much, I asked for help.
2. I was sent to Esalen, and I opened my heart and showed myself for the first time.
3. I was reflected back unconditional love.
4. I made a new association to drugs and vowed to start a new life.
5. I took action and started my new life.

I left Esalen to come home to my old life in Denver, and I was sober. I was working as an exotic dancer at the time, and I went to work the next day as I still had bills to pay, but this time I went sober. I saw the world I was living in, and I began to feel a deep sadness for the life I had created for myself. I tried to work, but kept feeling myself called to this new life I desperately wanted. So I made a decision. I was going to move to Esalen, and obtain all of the wisdom I could get, until I could learn how to create the life I wanted to live.

I went home after two weeks of work, packed up my car, got out of my lease, and drove to Big Sur. I lived, worked, studied, and transformed over the course of eight months living at Esalen. There were many, many experiences I went through. But for the purpose of this book, I'll stick to the key points. I loved Esalen, but it was also a bit busy for me. I love peace and quiet, and space. And when you live and work at Esalen, you live with another roommate in a small room, and everything else is shared community space. So after eight months I was ready to leave, and find a space of solace where I could learn more. I noticed a woman in the kitchen one day, asking for her own food in a special way, and I asked her what she was doing. She replied by sharing her experience from living at a Zen center in Ithaca New York, that ran a raw food detox for people who wanted to be physically healthy. I thought to myself, wow! I know nothing about how to take care of my body's health. I'll go there and work, and learn from new teachers!

Which is exactly what I did. I packed up my things, and went out to Ithaca as the new summer setup season was starting, and I began to serve under a Zen monk named David, and his Sufi wife, Marcia. I had landed in MY version of spiritual heaven. For the Zen center was nestled in the most beautiful land, and Marcia had cultivated the most beautiful landscape with her inner visions. My job was to work six hours a day doing food prep., or bathroom clean up, cleaning houses for the guests etc. In exchange, I was blessed with a beautiful tent all to myself in the woods. I had a full-sized bed, along with a dresser. I was in heaven!

The Zen center was called *Body Mind Restoration Retreats*, and I served there for three consecutive summers. David would guide us into the practice of Zen Buddhism, while we learned the blessing of selfless service to other beings. I would say that the Dharma teachings, along with being of service, were two main pillars inside my inner transformation. For it really solidified the inner-knowing that we are here to serve other beings, we are here to make ourselves into a whole being, to shine our brightest light possible so we may then shine that light for other beings that need help. Together we all form this kind of cosmic ladder, that then allows the whole planet to awaken and be served with wisdom, so we all may love one another and ourselves in a timeless manner.

We also had the opportunity to study with Marcia, and truly learn what food does to our body, what chemicals do to our body, and how all of that effects our long term health. How to eat, how to nurture our body, how to meditate, how to play, and how to care for the long-term health, was a key aspect of what we all learned. I had no idea up until that point that chemicals were being put in our food, and I got to see many guests come through the center. Some getting a diagnoses, being told they had only months to live, but after they detoxed and changed their diets, they lived years. Many magical things transpired while I watched how we really are what we eat, and how to make healthy food choices that serve my long-term health goals now.

I was studying the Dharma, making new friends, and learning more and more about what called to my heart. This is where I knew I wanted to help people, this was where my inner-spark awoke to nudge me into helping others wake up and heal, but first I knew I had to heal myself. Feeling inspired through the on site yoga teacher, who awakened a love so deep inside of my soul I can still feel it in my body when I close my eyes, I chose the path of becoming a yoga teacher. Not necessarily to teach, but I knew I had to deepen my spiritual healing in order to help others.

TAKE AWAY:

1. The food we put in our body does matter.

2. If I eat poorly, my body will have disease, if I have disease I won't be happy.

3. Selfless service is a birthright, and one which everyone deserves to experience.

4. Studying with Marcia and David is a timeless treat I will forever be grateful for.

5. I need to cultivate myself; evolve myself in order to truly be able to help others.

My next stop was Nosara, Costa Rica, where I spent every penny I had to attend a yoga teacher training with Don and Amba. These two bright lights guided us all through a one-month long, very intensive yoga teacher training, with an underlining message of this: *Follow your heart always.* They gave us the tools to safely guide and nourish the students, but also always encouraged us to come from our hearts, and honor our own unique version of their teachings. They encouraged us to awaken the unique gifts we were born with, and channel those through our yoga classes, and that's exactly what I did! I returned to the Zen center that following summer and became the yoga instructor. Feeling my nervous self blossom, I began to see what unique gifts I had been bestowed, and that's when I found out how tuned in I was to what wasn't being said, and how I could listen with my body to what other beings were really saying.

Truth is, before I went to Nosara, I made a choice to leave America for good! So before I left, I sold my car, and all my belongings so I would have money to start a new life in Nosara after the course ended. I would be a surfing, yoga teacher for the rest of my days. But my soul had other plans. After I finished the course, I knew in my heart Costa Rica was not my forever home, and I also had a tug in my heart that my journey was just beginning. So follow the heart tug I did, as I flew back to Colorado to prepare my next plan of action…

TAKE AWAY:

1. Cultivate yourself so you can serve others.

2. Become a master of what you love, then share what you love.

3. Your style is unique, and the gifts you have are only inside of you. If you choose to not share those gifts with the world, you're actually depriving the world of blessings.

4. Follow your heart, even if your plans change rapidly, and you have to move back to your hometown and borrow your brother's car. Always follow your heart with gusto, and always listen.

At this point, my family was beginning to ask me what my long-term plan was, which of course triggered me as I didn't have one. But what I did have, was a knowing that I wanted a spiritual life, and I wanted to help people. However, what I found was that when I tried to live off of being a yoga teacher, it was a tough racket. When I tried to live off of selling my art, that as well was a tough racket. Struggling was not my favorite, so I found a plan that entailed me raising my income, while still helping others. So I went to Crestone Colorado, to study massage therapy.

There was a town called Crestone, four hours south of Denver, population 2,000. It was where many Tibetan monks settled, and built temples after China came to take over Tibet, as the Tibetans found that the land in Crestone was very similar to the land in Tibet. You could feel it as well, even as you got close to the town. It was surrounded by the Sangre de Cristo Mountains, as well as the Great Sand Dunes National Park. Nagas lived in the valleys, and fairies claimed the creeks. Magic doesn't even begin to describe the happenings that went on inside of Crestone.

Dan and Sue opened their hearts and home to us students. There were eight of us about to spend a three-month period together to get our massage therapy certification, and hopefully leave with blossoming, well paying jobs!

This was no ordinary school. We were going to leave with massage certifications, but the true training took place inside of our souls. Every morning we participated in an hour of either Kundalini yoga or Chi-gong. Then breakfast, then class. It was rigorous to say the least. Dan held a space that was nothing short of light warrior-training camp. He found our hidden patterns, and brought them to the surface so we may step into our light, and reclaim our lives in a sacred way, while simultaneously helping others heal their bodies. The school was brutal. It was constant, and it stripped us of all we thought we knew about ourselves, then filled us back up with our own authenticity.

Truth be told, this is where I learned that trauma and pain in the body must be released for whole body healing. If one thinks they have an emotional issue around their father for example, and they also have subsequent chronic low back pain, this low back pain can be directly link to the father issues. Heal the father issues, heal the back pain. Heal the back pain, heal the father issues. They are one in the same. Another student could be working on me, and all of a sudden release a hidden trauma that I was holding in my body. Emotions would follow with the release, and then my entire life could transform. The interweaving of how complex we are as beings, is very, very expansive. Layer upon layer, we stack as we go through this trauma and that trauma, and then all of a sudden, we have low back pain, poor digestion, and chronic headaches. We try to treat the symptoms only, but that is a temporary exploration, not a permanent fix. We were taught that if we raise our vibrations through healthy eating, taking care of our spirit with yoga or meditation, and we enter into our healing sessions with that high vibration, we then invite our clients to raise to the vibration we set while we work on their bodies. Setting this up in time and space, allows one to have these profound emotional breakthroughs while their body is being healed, allowing them to have permanent healing in their bodies, minds, and emotions.

This wasn't a *lather up your client in oil and rub*, kind of school. This was the deepest of soul transformational schools. Dan pushed us hard. He wanted us to hit our edge, for it was at our edge we really found out our profound inner-strength. It is for this I will always be in a state of gratitude to him. He did show me how strong and capable I was, he did show me my profound gifts and how to use them. It was at this school I learned how to imprint with my mind.

I was the person Dan chose one day to use as an example while he was teaching Shiatsu. I lay on the ground face down while he went over the channels, and showed the whole class how to do that modality. He leaned over and said, "now Scarlet, you're going to receive, but you won't be able to watch. So make sure you stay present." Shiatsu was one of the hardest tests to pass with Dan, as the still point in the technique had to be truly authentic, and still, or he wouldn't pass you out of shiatsu training. And not passing is not a position you want to be in with Dan.

I began to pretend in my mind while he was working on me, that I was him. I was Dan teaching the class how to treat with Shiatsu, I had a perfect still-point and I was already in possession of the memorization of the pattern we were to travel through. Every time he pressed into my body, I saw it as myself pressing into myself. I felt my whole system glow as I had perfected this modality.

When it came time for us students to work on one another, Dan watched closely as I worked on my partner making sure that I understood most of what he said since I wasn't truly able to watch. He noticed as I moved through the Kata with ease, knowing all the points. He also noticed how my still-point was subtle and perfect. He looked at me and said, "Scarlet, how is it that you have picked this up so quickly when you didn't even see my demonstration?"

I explained to him that he told me I could do anything perfectly if I set my mind to it. So that's what I did. And I shared with him how I imprinted my being onto his, and rested in his very knowing of Shiatsu, and that's how I knew I knew it perfectly, as I took that imprint with me.

I don't know how I knew how to do this, I just did it and it worked, it wasn't until later I would find out what technique I was using and how perfectly I used it.

The word transformational doesn't even begin to describe my experience. It awakened parts of my being that were asleep for many lives, and the experience gifted me with a new certificate which could lead to having a rich career in helping others, which was my main goal.

TAKE AWAY:

1. Stay present, for in the present is where all the insight remains.
2. Take care of yourself with a spiritual practice, for this will raise your vibration and that vibration can then help others heal.
3. You can do anything you set your mind to.
4. You are here to help others evolve, it's that simple.
5. You are love, and you deserve love.
6. There is nothing that can take the place of incredible wisdom keepers, like Dan and Sue.

This is a walk through my path, which did not end in Crestone, by no means. I then traveled to Northern California, where I realized my rent would be tripled and I would be forced to integrate and apply all that I had been taught. The financial struggle was real. I had felt well informed on how to help others heal, however I felt leagues away from how to live a rich, abundant life. I had put a cap on my financial performance unknowingly, and it wasn't until three years later, when I went to a Bob Proctor conference in LA, that I had put together all I had learned with a practical application to reach the financial goals I had always dreamed of reaching.

I knew in my heart that if I always struggled to pay my bills, I would be giving a certain amount of my sacred energy to just that, and my ability to reach and help more beings would not be available. If I could raise my own pay rate to that where I lived in financial abundance, then I would be able to reach more people, be able to create more opportunities for others, and be able to reward myself for a job well done!

We are able to receive all the abundance this world has to offer, and a spiritual life does not mean a poor life. Wealth is nothing but energy, and in the hands of someone with beautiful intentions, wealth changes the world for the better. I took what I learned from Bob Proctor and Tony Robbins, and began to apply their concepts to my life. Once I did, it was like everything I had learned up until that point was being neatly organized in my mind, to allow me to step into abundance and allow me to reach more and more people on a daily basis!

For the first time, I was able to see how my mind and my view of my finances was creating that reality! All I had to do was change how I saw my financial abundance, make a decision, create a goal, then stop at nothing to achieve that goal! In the following chapters, I will go over more of these teachings. Teachings that have the ability to lay the groundwork for you to live a life of service, abundance, and a happy, happy soul!

CHAPTER FOUR:

Walking the Walk, the Universal Key to Getting Everything You Want in This Life

"The only limits in our life are those we impose on ourselves."

~ Bob Proctor

This chapter will be the most important chapter in this entire book by far. For this chapter will explain the key to truly understanding how to bring in anything you want into your life. The overall intention of this book is to lay a foundation for you to grasp how you ARE creating the status of your current health, and the way your life feels and looks to you is your creation as well. Self empowerment, and really grasping that you are a creator of your own reality, is a very empowering thought, and I hope it is for you also. When I state, "creator of your own reality" I am not referring to you or someone you know creating their own physical sickness, for life has a tendency to toss us challenges, to reflect back our own true strength. I am also not stating that if one was abused, they created that reality either. I am merely referring to the fact that we have the innate power to control how life looks FOR us, and this is our greatest power.

When we play the victim role, we are voluntarily giving our power away. When we curse others for what has happened to us in this lifetime, we are giving our power away. I am not standing here now without compassion for things that can exist in this world, for there are some terrible happenings to children, and other circumstances that we could examine and say, "how in the world is it okay that this happened to a person?"

Those circumstances do exist. And I am not condoning them by any means. But what we do have control over, is how we view what has happened to us. We can either remain a victim, or channel the trauma into something that creates strength within us, creates a platform for us to help and heal others, and take our power back by transmuting the bad into the good. That is the power we have within us, and that is also the choice we have to make every second of every day. Perspective.

If I were to go through and blame others for my inner-pain, everyone that I choose to blame, I am giving my power to. Another option would be that I sit with the pain. I channel it into a state of healing, and from that place of being healed, I then see the strength it gave me, the courage it gave me, and then the connection it allows me to have with other people that have been hurt in the same way. I can now sink into the depths with others, because I myself have been to those depths. I can empathetically feel what others sit in, and from that place, offer them the insight so they can then lift themselves out. Because I have been where they have been.

If my life had been a cushy, princess-style existence where everything was always taken care of for me, I never endured any abuse, never endured any pain, then what capacity would I really have to connect and help others? How would I be able to truly relate to their suffering if I myself have not endured any suffering? There would in fact be a layer of removed understanding, due to the fact that I have a lack of experience in having to help myself through the same issues. This my loves, is why we are here. We are here to heal ourselves, transmute the pain into courage, and help others to see the light. We are here to first clean up our own backyards, sculpt ourselves into God's highest form of creation, then use that cultivated inner-power to lift others from their pain and suffering. That ripple effect will then allow those you have helped to help others, and so on and so on, until the world is one big bright shining light!

So how do we do this? How do we create the life we want to live? How do we heal ourselves so that we can help others? What IS the key to this all happening?

There are two parts to our mind. One part is the conscious mind, and the other part is the subconscious mind. As human beings, we have thoughts all the time throughout the day, and these very thoughts are not just flashes through the ethers, they are substantial things in this world. For they are truly what has created your current reality. When a thought passes through the mind and it is connected to emotions, that powerful bolt of energy then shoots down into the subconscious mind, and programs the physical body with a feeling.

We know this, as I am sure you have had this experience many, many times. Let's say you just had a break up with your partner. You're sad and going through the emotions of losing someone you loved, even though you know the break up is for the best for both of you. You are trying to move through the pain, but you seem to be thinking of him or her every day. And every time you do think of that person, it creates a spark of feeling in your body. This pain of losing another being in your life, is a very charged feeling. This is an example of how your current programmed reality, is matched to your thoughts. If you were to go about your life in this way, always cycling through the loss of your partner, your body would remain in state of inner-pain, and what you would then attract into your life would be more pain. The antidote to this thought pattern would be to see the separation is for the best, be grateful for what your ex has given you, and begin to focus on the loving relationship you truly do want in your life. Every time the thought comes into your head around the loss of a love, give gratitude for what that person has given you, then re-direct your thoughts to the positive loving relationship you wish to call into your life.

This is training your mind. This is flexing the muscle of creating your own reality, and the beginning of training yourself to see things as happening for you, and not to you.

Another example would be a person who has accrued a lot of debt with his credit card. Every day he says to himself, "I wish I didn't have debt!" and in his body as his mind creates that thought, he feels the fear of not having enough money, and then the subconscious mind is imprinted with this feeling. And guess what is being pulled into his life? More debt! The antidote to this cycle would then be to train your mind, which you can do, to focus on what it is you DO want. And when you're training yourself to focus on this, you also add a sprinkle of imagination to bring in emotion with the new thought wave, so that it is then powerfully imprinted into the subconscious. What you will begin to attract into your life, is abundance, a huge savings account, and a life without credit card debt.

We as humans tend to focus on the very thing we fear, and we focus on that thing with the backing of emotional input, which is an alchemical recipe for the very things we do not want!

Well then Scarlet, what do we do you ask? I ask you to make a commitment here and now, to begin to re-train the way you live and think. Right here and now. I ask you to make a firm decision, that you will put energy into watching what you think. And when a negative thought arises in your life, you counter with a thought of something you do want, and then muster up the courage to feel this in your body.

There are times of grief in our lives, there are times when sadness overtakes us, and I am not saying one shouldn't grieve, or one shouldn't cry over a lost love, and really feel those emotions. Feeling one's own emotions while experiencing real grief, is very different then choosing to prolong that very grief by making the choice to think about it long since it's grief cycle has ended. Everyone has their own timeline for their grief cycle, and you're the only one that can tap into the timeline that best serves you. But my gut tells me you know when you're tipping into negativity, and you're choosing to rest in the drama because it's what you know, it's what you're comfortable with. It's nothing to be ashamed of, we all do it from time to time. It's part of the learning process of being human, and becoming a self empowered individual. Just my pointing this out to you will allow another level of your awareness to form, and when you do tip the scale from feeling what needs to be felt in a healthy way, to intentionally drawing it out past when it serves you, you'll now have an awareness that kicks on in your mind. Saying to yourself, "now, is this thought really serving me? Or is it time to move on?"

So here we are, learning how to create the life we want. Learning how to attract abundance, and vibrant health into our lives, and learning to watch what we think in order to make this happen. Our goal is to know how we are programming our subconscious mind, and this takes patience, compassion, and repetition…

For however many years you have been on this earth, your subconscious has been programmed. And until you develop the awareness on how you have done that, you're being programmed with many things that may or may not be serving you. For example, meet Belle. Belle was raised by a drunk father, and an absent mother. She never had anyone tell her she was smart, or beautiful, and she certainly never felt loved by those around her. She was a bright little girl, but her teachers also called her stupid, due to the fact it was hard for her to concentrate and pay attention in school, as no one taught her how to do that either.

By the time Belle is 18, she moves to a new city, and gets a job at a grocery store as a check out girl. Here she works day in and day out, hearing the beep of a product being scanned, thinking to herself that she isn't pretty, she isn't smart, and she is lucky to have this menial job to pay her rent in her 400 square-foot studio apartment that's dark and dismal. She doesn't have many friends, and she thinks to herself, "Why would anyone want to be my friend? I am not even smart, and I have nothing to offer."

If Belle was to take the perspective that life happened to give her, that she was told she isn't' anything therefore she isn't anything, then she would be giving her power to those around her that tried to knock her down. If she takes the perspective of knowing that she doesn't like how she feels about herself, and she knows she wants change, she will begin the path to figuring out how to have self-esteem and create a million-dollar income in her life. But the key fact to this story is, it's up to Belle. It's not up to her drunk father, it's not up to her ignorant teachers, it's up to her. Her drunk father, and ignorant teachers were actually pillars of teachings for her to overcome and test her strength, if she chooses to view these instances as such.

So Belle decides there must be more in this life. She begins to read self-help books, and they start to make her feel better for a short period of time. But eventually she falls back into the feeling of helplessness, and she gives up once again.

Belle's subconscious mind has been programmed for years that she is worth nothing! For years she has heard from external people that she is nothing, and she has believed them! She began to parrot to herself in her mind, with her thoughts, that she was nothing, which then created a horrible feeling in her body of sadness and despair. Then her life unfolded in a sad, desperate fashion. It is this simple folks, it is this simple. If you only take one thing away from this book, I ask that you to take this formula into your life with a conviction, stronger than your greatest desire. Your thoughts are creating your reality!

Just having this awareness in your mind as we speak, is changing how you see your life, and raising your awareness. For this insight is the key to drawing to you what you want in this life. Now, there are certain steps that MUST be taken and must not be taken lightly. For we all have years of negative imprints we must re-write. And for most of us, this isn't going to happen overnight. That is why I ask you to make a commitment to yourself, and the future generations to come. That you commit to watching your thoughts, generating positive thoughts of things you do want in your life, and allowing emotions to follow suit. This practice must be done on a daily basis, and it must be done with compassion.

We live in a world now where things happen so quickly, that the new generations come through and want things to happen overnight. We want to heal overnight! We want a pill we can take just once, to fix all of our problems. And we have lost touch with the beauty of earnest hard work that happens over time, to create lasting solid results. If you enter into this formula with an earnest mindset, knowing you'll choose to be compassionate to yourself when things don't happen overnight, but know deep in your heart that you're going to begin building a new life for yourself from the ground up, and it's a worthy endeavor, it WILL work.

Small goals leading to one massive end goal, is the design here. So let's get started!

Take a moment to figure out what your end goal is, and may I suggest that you take the lid of what you THINK you can have, earn, and feel like, and really just sink into your imagination of what it is you want in a fantasy realm or this realm.

If I were to ask Belle what she wanted to earn in a year, she would probably go to her logical mind and think, "well I earn $20,000 a year now, but $50,000 a year would make me way more happy and comfortable." I would say to Belle that she has just capped her potential, that she has just sunk into her vision of her current self-worth and given an answer from that place, rather than removing through the imagination all of the limits you have put upon yourself, and really brew from the limitless space of your heart. WHAT DO YOU WANT? You're a limitless being, and it's about time you started to think like one.

So from this limitless space, take a separate sheet of paper (or go to www.scarletravin.com and print out the workbook for this book) and answer this question, what is your goal? That one dream you have always had, it can relate to your health, your wealth, attracting the perfect partner, anything. Write this goal down on this paper in the present tense, like you have already achieved the goal, and you're currently resting in what it would feel like to be in the world where this goal has been manifested. Once it's written, re-read it to yourself with FEELING. Imagine you're telling your closest friend. Speak it with feeling!

I speak my goal into a recording, and first thing when I wake up, I listen to this recording. I tell my age so I have a timeline for it's manifestation, and I also speak to how it all feels while I have it. I speak every word with conviction and passion, and I even incorporate external people, and speak to how proud they are of me, or how happy others are for me! I love creativity. I love using my imagination, and I love training my imagination with such a worthy legitimate practice that will enhance my life and the lives of others.

What I just described in this practice, is imprinting the subconscious mind. It takes a definite decision to do this twice a day. I do it once in the morning, and once at night. It takes persistence to continue to repeat yourself on a daily basis, and to not give up when you don't see the results unfolding before your very eyes! You must commit! You must follow through, and when you're feeling like you want to give up, that's when you must try even harder! For that very feeling of giving up, is the old you trying to pull you back, while the new you is begging to be born. Give that new you a chance at survival. See your life as worthy, as I see your life and know that the gift that is waiting to be born in our very essence is something this world needs, and you're the only one who can offer it. If it helps you to push through this while thinking that it will eventually serve others, then use that as motivation! If it helps you to think of manifesting a larger house so your dog has a huge yard to play in, use that as motivation!

The key to this all working, and work it will, I can guarantee that, is repetition. And never, and I mean never, give up. For your journey is now just beginning, and the task at hand will get easier and easier as you begin to watch your life change right before your eyes. But you must give 110%. You must do this daily, and twice daily. And you must know that your very place in this world, is to master your own domain. To bring to yourself whatever it is you want, and master the key that connects you to the infinite intelligence. That master key is your subconscious.

I personally found that mastering persistence was what I needed to be successful. I found that many of my comrades would try this fad or that fad and when it didn't work, they would simply give up, be stagnant for a spell, then go for the next fad. All they really needed to do was to make a commitment to what it is they want in their life, then go for it! No excuses!

You'll begin to feel a tinge of self empowerment arise as you start to follow through with this practice. And the knowing that once you set your main goal, the universal intelligence will vibrationally connect with the program you have just fed your subconscious mind, and begin to unfold the path before your very eyes to bring in what it is you're seeking. I am not kidding here. This will happen. It's not a theory, it's not some *woohoo* spiritual gimmick. It's the very law of the universe, and this very law has been used by the 1% income earners of this nation for decades.

Why do you think 1% of our population earns 99% of the income in the US? These people have learned this very secret, and they have learned how to train their minds, therefore training their subconscious and therefore bringing in the life they desire. The more money they have, the more people they can help, and I know deep within your heart that you want to help others, for that's a universal soul calling.

Discouragement can arise, for it's the negative part of your perspective that you're used to taking, looking for what's wrong rather than looking for what's right. And trust me, you can see whatever it is you want to see, that's how powerful you are. So as we are re-training ourselves on how to live an incredibly rich life, it's also helpful to make small weekly goals that we can accomplish on a smaller scale, and then reward ourselves for accomplishing them, in turn building our self-esteem. (Which is crucial to all forms of success) and also helping climb the ladder to our end goal.

A small weekly goal could be, I am going to put in one hour daily towards moving towards my end goal. What does that look like? For me, that would look like putting one hour each day towards working on my self-esteem, and practices that sink me into the knowing that I AM God's form of highest creation, and I am able to create the life I want to live. I'll go over my rituals now in short, but also know I have resources on my website explaining these practices in more depth. There is also a workbook available for downloading on my website to help walk you through this practice of knowing yourself, and your goals in a deeper way on a daily basis.

I wake up, and I write ten things I am grateful for in the present tense. These are things I want in my life, but don't have yet. I write them all in the present tense like I already have them, and I FEEL what it would feel like to have them. I am imprinting and re-training my subconscious mind. Then I read one chapter from a book that speaks to the power of thinking, *Think and Grow Rich*, by Napoleon Hill. I read one chapter of this book every morning, and I never stop. So once I finish the book, I simply go right back to the beginning, and begin to read it again and I have to say, I always get more and more out of this book every time. And again, I am imprinting my subconscious with material that supports the knowing that I am creating my reality, therefore leading to self empowerment, and therefore attracting into my life everything my heart desires. I then listen to my recording on my end goal, and feel everything I speak on, imprinting my subconscious.

I then sit up, and do my twenty-minute *transcendental meditation*, which is unwinding the physical stress in my body, strengthening my mental clarity, allowing me to rest in a more peaceful state, so when I do my manifestations I am not riddled with the overwhelming feelings of my past traumas. For through the practice of TM, I am able to relate to my past in a more neutral way, and a great sense of peace builds in my system as I practice. This morning ritual can take 1-2 hours depending on the length of chapter in *Think and Grow Rich*.

I made a decision. I made a commitment to myself, and I followed through on a daily basis. This ritual, which Tony Robbins states, "we are defined by our rituals," is bringing me closer and closer to what I aim for in my life. It seems strange to me that many people in this world want things, but don't want to work on themselves to get them. They want more money, they want better health, they want a wife, or a husband but they don't work on the very thing that is going to bring that to them. They don't work on themselves. Most of us wake up, we go to work at a job we think is just "ok" then we come home, tired. We numb out with tv, complain about our life, then go to bed. You WILL have to focus on yourself, to change yourself, to heal yourself. You WILL have to begin with small tasks everyday that works towards the whole. You need the will, and the will is born from you. I cannot give it to you. I may be able to inspire you to make change, but the follow through is all on you. So I ask you now, how bad do you want change? How bad to you want that ocean front mansion? How bad do you want your health issues to subside? The strength to which you truly want change, will be the direct connection with how hard you try to get it. So dig deep, find what drives you, and harness that power. Whether it be for the love of a woman, the drive to make your parents proud, the drive to leave your children a legacy, the drive to help others in this world and to end the suffering of the people. Dig deep into your soul, and tap into this drive and make it so. Do the work and come out on top.

Everyone is also starting from a different place, and some may, at first, need the assistance of a coach or counselor to be guided through the pain and trauma that is holding them back, and for this I do offer resources in the back of this book so you know without a fraction of a doubt, that you will be helped, and guided back into your own inner-strength. There is never a task too large, never a dream too big, and never a goal that cannot be reached. Like Les brown states, "Shoot for the moon. Even if you miss you'll land among the stars." What I have to add to that is "once you land among the stars, you'll be even closer to the moon, so reset that goal and go for Pluto!"

CHAPTER FIVE:

Awakening Self Empowerment: Cultivate Yourself and the Rest Will Follow

"Everything in life that tests your limits is here to show you that you are limitless."

~ Scarlet Ravin

Let us begin by baking a personal self empowerment cake! The ingredients we will need are compassion, drive, decision-making abilities, persistence, imagination, love and a huge scoop of faith to go right on top. These are not just words that I just typed before you, they are vibrational representations of what one needs to integrate fully inside of themselves to step into a sense of deep self empowerment.

Let's first get on the same page. When I speak of self empowerment, I am directly referring to the inner-sense and knowing that you have everything you need within yourself to manifest, heal, and create whatever it is your true heart desires. Along with the knowing that you are complete and perfect unto yourself, just as you are now. The teachings and inspirations I have been offering in this book, are just sheer mirrors to awaken what it is you already have within you. You are not obtaining anything new here, you are reading words which awaken that which is already inside of your own being, because your being as it rests in this moment is whole, perfect, and God's form of highest creation.

Awakening to this knowing is the goal here, and this goal to have as one's chief aim in life, is to me, the highest form of a goal, because it is the key to unlock all of your inner-potential, and to know without a fraction of a doubt that you are perfect! I would also invite you to join me in a new definition of perfect, as this universe has quite skewed versions of that word. In my heart, perfect is authenticity. It's the direct expression of your TRUE INNER SELF. It's the outward stroke of what wants to be expressed on the inside, if your heart is telling you to dance in the rain to feel alive, and yell at the top of your lungs that you love water, then that's just perfect. If it means that you must break up with your boyfriend because your needs are not being met, then that's just perfect.

Having a filter of self empowerment as you view what others think you should be or should do, will release you from what they think is perfect for you, and what is perfect for you and allow you to express yourself in direct relation to your own authenticity. Wait, it gets even better, your true authenticity is something that comes from your very soul, so no other being on this planet will have more insight than yourself on how you need or should express yourself. In fact, if someone has a suggestion of how you need to change to fit their version of what is "perfect," then they are just choosing to project their own inner-struggles and limitations onto your outward expressions. Which, in turn, blocks your own authenticity, which in turn dampens your soul and leads to a deep inner sense of sadness. Nod your head if you feel me.

I have been in relationships time and time again in my younger years where the men I was with, were always making small suggestions of how I should change myself in order to fit their version of what is perfect, or what is best for me. When I was less aware of my own self empowerment, I would willfully listen and curtail my expressions to fit their vision. I would try it on so to speak, and eventually, little by little my soul would dampen. If I continued this inauthentic dance, then the slight dampening would eventually turn into anger, which I would then direct out at my boyfriend, when truly I was just mad at myself for not honoring my very own truth!

As you can see, as humans we have many layers to dive into, to find our true authentic selves. As we have grown from baby to adult, we have been flushed with so many external beliefs that when we are adults and it comes time to figure out who we are on our own two feet, we literally have to strip away all that we thought we know, to figure out all that we truly are. This is why I spent fifteen years traveling the planet, sitting with this teacher and that teacher to find myself. For all the teachers were just mirrors that rested before my soul, and awakened myself to deeper, inner-visions of who I was, in my authentic presence. We must know who we are on the deepest soul level, to be authentic within ourselves, and our own lives. And we must have this knowing before we can enter into a state of self empowerment.

I spent fifteen years searching for what I was at a core level, and I'll let you in on my findings. Perhaps if you can take this in at a soul level, you will be able to shorten your journey of self-discovery, and enter right into the knowing of it. The secret, to what you truly are, at your very core... YOU ARE LOVE. You are not your pain, you are not your reflections onto others, you are not how others think you are, or what your parents told you that you were. You are sheer, unconditional undeniable love. This is you at your core. This is your authentic state of being, and this is what you are when you walk through your day-to-day happenings. To hear me speak this to you, and for you to truly grasp this at your core are two different things, that is true.

Adding a daily mantra to your ritual of self-development saying, "I am love. My authenticity is unconditional love," is a very helpful start to integrating this knowing to the very core of your being. Let's pause to really soak this in, and I want you to take a moment from reading any further until you sit, close your eyes, and say in your heart, "I am Love." Say it over and over until you begin to feel the awakening of this knowing. If it doesn't come right away, then know it's now time to put into practice self-compassion, for your being has some layers that are asking to be seen, and it is the duty of your being to push through these layers and discover yourself truly. This is a very worthy goal indeed, for it will unlock all of your hidden potential, and allow you to truly shine brighter and brighter in this world. And as another being on this planet, that is all I could have ever asked for and hoped for from you, to shine! Shine from the inside out, show me who you truly are, walk through this life with an authenticity that shakes awakenings in other human beings! If you walk this plane with a true authenticity, you will be inspiring others to awaken with your very presence. Many think we HAVE to make big ideas come to fruition to change and heal the planet, when truly we just have to discover our true nature, and the rest will follow suit.

As an empathetic woman, I was given the gift of feeling the unaligned nature of other humans around me. I grew up feeling many things that I had no idea weren't my own. But as I began to cultivate this gift more and more (and I am still cultivating this gift, for it's an evolutionary process that will never end) I feel when someone is not in alignment with their true nature, and I feel how disarming it is for me to be able to converse with them. Funny enough, horses have this very same gift, and I grew up with horses being my best friends. So we have counseled one another on how hard this is to be around, and I am grateful for their support in how to figure out how to deal with other people's in-authenticity. How did I deal with it? Well, with compassion of course!

Here is a beautiful story of a woman named Grace, who was not in alignment with her authentic nature during an equine therapy retreat.

Grace had just signed up for an equine therapy weekend. She had set the intention to discover her true calling in this life, and was really looking forward to getting more insight into why her life was not quite unfolding for her the way she had truly desired. The weekend was guided by a woman who had a couple of horses and a round pen, and the goal was going to be set into motion allowing the participant to enter into the round pen with the horse, and have the horse perform certain duties guided by the workshop leader.

Easy enough, Grace thought. Yet, she had not made the connection as to how this would connect her to her true life calling. The goal was to make Charley, the horse, trot around the round pen, then change directions and trot in the opposite direction. Grace who had spent maybe an hour around horses her whole life, felt a little nervous, but was up for the challenge. The workshop leader, we will call her Sara, asked Grace to stand in front of the round pen and set her intention as to what she was going to have Charley do. She then repeated the instruction of trotting in both directions, then entered the round pen with her lunging whip, and stood in the center of the pen while Charley dug around for snips of grass to eat, paying no mind to Grace at all.

As Grace began to make her first motion to get Charley to start walking in her chosen direction, the rest of the participants noticed that Grace asked, "Charley, walk!" and Charley with his large behind facing Grace, did nothing but search for more grass. With a building sense of frustration, as Grace had just previously watched two other workshop participants perform the task at hand with Charley listening perfectly, began to feel sorry for herself, and therefore exerted more force on Charley, raising her voice and flailing the lunge whip. Charley felt her shift in energy, which went from a timid field mouse, to a large mountain dragon in two seconds, and began to gallop around the round pen, even kicking his heels up to shake off her whirlwind energy. Now Grace had to figure out how to get Charley from a gallop to a trot, as was her original intention.

She began to yell, "Charley trot! Whoa!" and Charley, not understanding still what Grace wanted, continued to gallop around the round pen. With external guidance coming forward, Sara the workshop leader began to counsel Grace, "Grace, I want you to feel what it would feel like in your body to have Charley trot. What does that energy feel like to you? What does it feel like to see and know Charley is trotting? What kind of calming energy do you need to feel inside your own heart to exert this inner-vision?"

Grace began to close her eyes, feel in her heart what it would feel like to see Charley trotting, and what her energy had to feel like to match this speed for him. As she began to sink into this authentic, inner-feeling, Charley began to trot around the round pen while Grace's eyes were still closed. As Grace opened her eyes, she noticed Charley trotting and felt a deep sense of gratitude.

When it came time to change direction for Charley and trot in the other direction, Grace first felt into the core of her being what this expression would externally look like, then she softly began to outwardly express this action towards Charley, and of course Charley willingly responded.

Horses read your authenticity, they don't respond to your words or your flailing expressions. They feel what you feel at your core and run off of that message. They are a perfect tuning fork to know what it is you're truly expressing from the inside out. As many times for most of us, we are so far removed from who we truly are at our very core due to years and years of putting on masks and not dealing with inner-pain, that we have become separated from our true authentic selves.

As a human with the same reading abilities, I have found it most difficult to be around people that are not operating from their true authentic natures. For what they say, does not energetically align with how they truly feel, and this very misalignment will send mixed feelings into my heart. Those mixed feeling leave me in a sheer inner-state of confusion, which leads to me not being able to believe the person, and what they are saying. I am not saying these people are liars, as most of them are not even aware of what they are doing, I am just saying that I know when one isn't in alignment, and this knowing produces a drive inside of me to inspire the people before me to awaken to their true nature. For once they do, they can express themselves in an unstoppable way getting what they truly want out of life!

For it's not just me or horses that respond in a confused matter to the inner-authentic, self-misalignment. The universe responds in the same fashion if your true inner-essence is convoluted with layers of pain, suffering, and masks one has created to remove them from who they authentically are at their core. Which is why is it imperative that we walk into the knowing of who we are, then express that through self empowerment. Without this being how we operate on a daily basis, the world will continue to feel like a struggle, and your gifts will continue to be disregarded by yourself.

Now knowing what we know to make a cake filled with self empowerment and authenticity, what do we do? We begin to make decisions from our own inner-truth rather than what we think others think we should do. We begin to tune into what is true for us every second of every day. We do this with compassion and understanding, as we start to birth ourselves anew from how we have been living in the past, to how we want to authentically live now. Some of us may need a life coach or guide to begin to reflect to us what it is we think we cannot see, and some may be able to practice insights from this book and get there on their own. Not one path is better or worse, everyone is just on their own path, and their own path is perfect for them.

First, we must make a clear decision that self empowerment is our goal, and through the firm clear decision to carry out this goal we understand that we must first tap into who we are. What are we empowering, and what pain or confusion do we need to authentically examine to reach our end goal of self empowerment?

I have on my website a worksheet, that is downloadable for you to fill out to align with where you are at now, and then use this as a marker in time to see who you are yet to become. Which isn't to say who you are yet to become is something separate from who you are now, but it is the expansion of what is already inside of you. You have just yet to awaken to this state of awareness.

Once we have made a clear decision to enter into a state of self empowerment, the universe will guide us through circumstances that will awaken this inside of ourselves. All we have to do is activate faith in this knowing, and if you don't believe me right off the bat then fake it until you make it, because it will come!

Another insight around this subject is knowing that you are not damaged, you are not broken, and you don't need fixing. The issues that you perceive as issues in your life are just moments that have come to light where your evolution is being tried. We need instances of growth to spark in us the insight to see our true power. If everything was just given to us, and everything was *easy peasy lemon squeezy*, then we would never know our true inner-strength. We would never know how much light we have inside of ourselves, and how beautiful we are! We would never know the beauty of overcoming a difficulty, or getting through a trauma! These are beautiful moments of insight and strength, and they are the soul food to our very state of evolution, and the gaining of awareness!

As Tony Robbins said, "The biggest problem you all have is the fact that you think you shouldn't have problems!" and he is right! A "problem" is just an event occurring in your life, that your soul has manifested on some level to test your strength. Cultivate self empowerment, then use this developed strength to help others! It's you training course on this walk called life ,to sculpt yourself into a warrior! To test your limits in order to know that you are truly limitless! Without these beautiful tests, one wouldn't know their strength, and we would simply move through this world as a sleepwalker!

I know how it feels when you see someone you love in pain, and I know the first instinct is to try to remove that pain from the person you love, or help them to exit the struggle they have created for themselves. And in a sense, that is my very goal of this book. But I also intend to walk the fine line of knowing that pain is also fuel for evolution. If I were to try to remove the pain and suffering from all the beings around me, then I would also be removing the very thing that is going to evolve them. I would be taking away their life lesson on strength and awareness. There is a balance in this, for if someone is being abused of course we want to step in and help out.

An example of this would be the following:

There is a couple and they are dating for a course of seven months. Through this time period, she longs for deeper love from him, and sees him as this amazing man who could be her husband one day. She puts 110% into the relationship (because if you're not doing that with everything you do in life, then what are you doing?) She tries to plan trips and adventures, and loves him every second with massages and making him meals. On the other side, the man is not sure if he loves the woman. Even though she is amazing and successful, he just isn't sure. He puts more energy towards his work, towards his friends, and never commits to going on trips and adventures with her, as it's not his priority. Eventually the woman feels a lack of his energy going into the relationship and speaks up for herself, asking for more. The man then responds by telling her he isn't sure he even loves her, and therefore doesn't want to give her more, and thinks they should stop dating. Heartbroken, the woman goes home to heal her heart, and resolve the inner-pain of being in love, and not having the man return the love.

Just two weeks later, the man reaches back out and expresses that he didn't know what he had until he lost it. Now he sees how he wasn't really showing up in the relationship, but was just thinking of himself most of the time, not considering her and what she was giving. The woman, thinking this means he is going to change and win her back, starts to feel her inner-hope and love reawaken, and steps out of the pain he had just caused her, and tries to love him once again. However, the man has yet to truly change.

Just two days after he has expressed his insight, he goes right back to saying that he is still not sure if he loves her, and needs time to figure out his own inner-life. Heartbroken once again, and this time feeling betrayed in a whole new way, the woman cuts him out of her life once and for all, releasing him to his own inner-workings, as he has made it clear he has no ability to be authentic with her. He is so unclear within himself and that must come before any serious relationship will ever evolve for him. It's most painful for her to cut him out of her life, and for the man to hear this strong decision of not being able to have this woman in his life, he falls to the floor in deep-seated pain, not knowing how this all even unfolded.

This very pain that is now growing inside of his being, will be the very fuel that may spark him to change and treat other woman differently in the future. It is an opportunity that can fuel him to gain insight into how to be authentic with women, how to take care of women, and show up with the same 110% as she did. Of course, his first job before he even has a chance to show up for a woman in a beautiful way, is to be clear first within himself. To know his heart truthfully, so that when he is involved with a woman, he can show up fully and know what he wants clearly. This is a beautiful lesson for him, and one that can really evolve his inner awareness of how his inner-confusion affects those around him in a negative way. If the woman were to reach back out and console him, she would be taking away the very fuel he needs to push him out of this pattern. So in this case, pain is good. It's fuel, and it will show the man his ability and strength!

This is just one example of how pain can be a catalyst, and how allowing the other to cycle through their own lessons, and seeing it as just that, is actually a beautiful perspective to adopt.

In the following chapter I will dive more into what can stop us from becoming self-empowered beings, and what it is we need to watch for on the path to knowing our true authenticity. What it looks like when we give our power away, and the detriment it has to our very soul when we do this. Always remember, it's the unseen in this world that holds the power, the seen is limited by whatever perspective we choose to adopt in that very moment. It can deceive us, or empower us, but how we choose to view the world will color our inner-selves. If we choose to take the perspective of self empowerment and that the world is happening *for* us and not *to* us, then we will begin to lead a very fulfilling life indeed.

CHAPTER SIX:

The Possible Road Blocks that May Shatter Your Dreams

"Pain, Pleasure and Death are no more than a process for existence. The revolutionary struggle in this process is a doorway to intelligence."

~ Frida Kahlo

I have found on my journey through the ages, that obtaining insight into what can evolve my being is very helpful, but what I have found even more helpful than gaining insight, is realizing awareness around what may stop me from achieving my goals, and what may hinder my growth. If I have awareness around these possible roadblocks, when they arise I can immediately recognize them, and stop them dead in their tracks, changing my due course from one of wreckage to one of victory. I dedicate this chapter to those inner fears, the outward expressions of those inner fears, and other obstacles that may tug at you, trying to keep your old self alive while the new incredible you seeks to be born.

The first roadblock we are going to recognize together is negative inner self-talk, and it can be an outward expression as well. If you are a human being, then you have experienced negative self-talk. That's the small or large voice inside your head that calls you stupid, strange, a loser, and many other words that don't line up with your true inner-nature. This negative self-talk is derived from fear, and fear is something that one can shirk if they are so willing. This can be very detrimental indeed, calling oneself anything but amazing, for when the repetition of thought inside your head is negative, then you are imprinting your subconscious mind with a negative image of yourself. You then spark that emotion inside your being as well, and you will then attract alignment with all that negativity into your life. Sounds awful right?

It's happening every day to millions of beautiful beings, sweet beings and sleepwalkers. It's happening mostly due to lack of awareness on how this affects our lives! Education around our thoughts and how we think of ourselves, is one that is lacking in schools. But the amazing part of this is that it is never too late to change how you speak to yourself, and treat yourself.

One bright and sunny day on Jenny's tenth birthday, surrounded by all the friends in her fifth-grade class, Jenny blew out her birthday candles.

The wax dripped down onto the cake as all of the children salivated, waiting for their slice of sweet-tooth cake! Jenny had made a wish that Taylor would hold her hand since it was her birthday, and she was in love with him. As the slices of cake were being passed out to each child, Jenny kept her sight on Taylor, waiting for him to gaze in her direction. But of course, as a boy at the age of ten, gazing into the eyes of a girl who perhaps had *coodies*, was the last thing on his mind. Jenny waited. Taylor kept eating and playing with the other boys. Finally, Jenny mustered up the courage to just go right over to him and ask to hold his hand, in fact how could he not? It WAS her birthday, and there was love between them. She could feel it, so how could he not?

Jenny left her spot at the head of the table and walked timidly over to Taylor. "Hi Taylor, do you want to hold my hand today?" she asked in front of her other classmates, in a very brave tone. Taylor took one look around at the other boys sitting next to him, and out of HIS fear of feeling vulnerable, he made a joke at Jenny's expense saying, "I don't hold girls hands. They have coodies!"

The entire class began to laugh at the fact that Jenny may in fact have coodies, and Jenny, with a broken heart, sulked back to her spot at the head of the table and began to push her cake around her plate, no longer feeling hungry. From that day on, Jenny's inner self-talk went from one of hope and dreams, to one of negativity. Her ego had been bruised, and her dreams of holding Taylor's hand crushed her heart, for what seemed like would last forever. She began to call herself stupid for seeking to hold Taylor's hand. She began to see herself as ugly. For what other reason would this boy do this to her?

That negative self-talk began to grow inside of Jenny's being, for she had no awareness of how she was imprinting her subconscious mind. And as she continued down this path, her body resonated with the negative self-talk, and her outward life's expression mirrored this self-disapproval.

Now Jenny is 36, and she still lingers on negative self-talk. She wonders why she has no long-lasting relationships and only dates jerks, and wonders why her opinion of herself is so low. She doesn't understand that she needs to watch very carefully how she speaks to herself, on the inside. She doesn't understand how to change the inner self-talk to positive self-talk so that her self-confidence may grow, and her true inner-light can begin to shine once more, leaving a huge imprint on this world as she was meant to do in the first place.

What do you think to yourself? What do you call yourself? What goals do you talk yourself out of accomplishing? And when did this negative self-talk begin? Most likely, it began when you were a child, and you made some silent decision to agree with the immaturity of the reflections around you, rather than maintaining the inner-knowing that you're perfect, you're beautiful, and anyone that can't see that in you is just living in their own fear of vulnerability and their own self-disapproval. Fortunately, now you have the information to change this, and with this information now in your awareness, you have just to call upon changing the thoughts in the moment on a daily basis until it becomes easier, and easier and easier. It may feel at first that you're faking it, that when you call yourself beautiful and amazing you don't really agree with this, but keep at it. Eventually you'll replace the negative with the positive, and soaring will be your only next option. Have compassion, for you may have a deep inner-wound that needs healing, and through this act of positive self-talk and self-love, you'll begin to heal that wound, and begin to unwind your authentic nature until it is showing itself to the world. Take back your power from your past pains, and become the hero of your own life. The time is now!

Now that you're loving yourself with your inner-words, the outward expression of this inner-love is taking care of the skin suit your soul is residing in, your body. This vessel, if cared for properly, will take you to great heights. Heights you never even conceived of imagining you could obtain, but it all starts with knowing yourself. How can you truly care for something you don't understand?

This, my loves, is a journey all to itself. For caring for your body will be a life-long journey of getting to know your very soul in more clear, and cosmic ways. There is no one-size-fits-all approach for me to share with you on how to care for the physical nature of your system, but I can share some pointers that you can hear, and then tailor to your own personal needs. You are the only one that knows the true essence of your own personal needs. This is also why taking a journey to see a doctor when one is sick is only half of the journey, the other half is filtering what the doctor suggests and then applying what YOU think is best for YOU.

Kindness and compassion towards yourself is the emotional starting point for caring for yourself, and setting the intention of loving your body and health will also carry you into this journey on the right path. Are you eating healthy? Are you aware of what is actually in your food? Have you done health and wellness research? (I will also give references in the back of this book as to locations where one can go and learn these teachings) Do you meditate? Do you retire to bed when your body is tired, or do you stay up with friends partying, knowing that it isn't going to serve your end goal? Are you taking drugs or drinking to numb out from deep-seated pain? Are you drinking enough water and exercising your body? Taking a moment to answer these questions on a separate sheet of paper will allow your awareness to locate yourself and where you are on this scale. Then once you have obtained that awareness, you can move forward with an action plan.

Taking small steps on a daily basis to get enough rest, to expose your senses to enlivening forces of nature, to feed your body with healthy and vibrant food, and to encourage yourself to sweat and move will end up putting your physical system on the same plane as your mental system. This recipe is unstoppable when it comes to obtaining that end goal you're seeking in regards to your health, and manifesting your dreams.

Another aspect to be aware of is whom you are surrounding yourself with. Our system will resonate with the six people we spend the most time with in our lives. Now knowing this, are you surrounding yourself with vibrant, goal driven, honest, loving, encouraging people? Or are you surrounding yourself with stagnant, sleepwalking, negative speaking people? The choice is yours. And always remember, you don't owe anyone in this world anything. If you truly tune into your heart, and sink into the space of love for yourself, when you close your eyes, are the people surrounding you really serving you? You making the choice to perpetuate what doesn't serve you also allows them to stay in a state of stagnation. Many times over I have heard the excuse from clients, "Well I have known them for twenty years, I can't just not be their friend." Then I respond by asking, "Does their presence bring you down? Or does it lift you up?" They reluctantly respond with, "Mostly bring me down, because I'm trying to change but they are just staying the same. It's sad really."

In these scenarios, one person has chosen to grow, to evolve, and to change. The other person has decided to stay stagnant, and even decline. The inner-obligation from the person who wants to change, keeps them stuck. So where did this obligation come from? Always good to keep in mind, that we are all made of energy. Energy cannot stay the same. It can either evolve and grow, or decline. So if you're not working on growing and evolving, then you're going backwards. It's really that simple.

As humans, we have a very skewed vision of what it can mean to love and support another person, and many of us are simply driven by the fact that we don't want to experience pain. In fact, we sacrifice ourselves and others to the sheer idea that we are trying to avoid pain. This is a totally different feeling than love and support, yet we continue to confuse the two. Everyone already knows in their heart when it is time to leave old friends, and even separate themselves from family members, due to the fact that the impact they are having on themselves is a very negative one. But due to the fact that they fear what they perceive as hurting another person, they continue to perpetuate the same pattern, even after they know it's hindering their very growth.

Just having this realization will allow you to choose another perspective around how you choose, and see the people in our life and whom you are surrounding yourself with. It's your choice, make no mistake about it, you don't owe anyone anything, but you do owe yourself to be honest, kind, loving, and driven to evolving your soul to the highest form in this life. And if that is truly your mission, you will begin to be able to view these life shifts differently. Instead of viewing them as hurting others by leaving them, or staying with others by hurting yourself, you'll see the shift as a growth opportunity and through the pain and struggle comes great strength and drive! Could there be anything better then putting yourself into a situation that encourages you to be stronger? Encourages you to be more driven? And encourages you to be your own best advocate choosing to only surround yourself with individuals on the same resonance as yourself, or even a higher resonance?

Know this in your mind now. Pain = Growth. Struggle = Change. Honoring oneself = Courage. In what universe are these attributes negative? For they are not. Our perception of them is, and our perceptions can be changed at any instant, that's how magical and creative it truly is to be human!

Many times over, I have seen the pain transition before my eyes, where one person struggles to leave old friends, and fear of the unknown combined with not wanting to hurt anyone, steps in. Once they make the decision and walk through that pain with a warrior attitude, they begin to see the shifts that unfold before their eyes. They begin to see just how detrimental the friendship is, and then they even begin to move so much higher in resonance that they can't even imagine how they stayed in the friendship or relationship as long as they did! They begin to marvel at the fact that it took them so long to walk away from something that was so toxic for them. Every human being on this planet is responsible for himself or herself, it is not your responsibility to change, heal and shift the lives of others. It is YOUR responsibility to change, heal and shift your own life with the inspiration that walking this walk will INSPIRE those around you to make their own changes, but you yourself can never change another person, they have to do that for themselves. So make a choice right here and now, to release yourself from having negative energies surround you, and make a commitment to surround yourself with six people of higher vibration or a resonating vibration, and allow your soul to soar!

I do believe that the true fear that humans have is not in what they fear they are never going to become, but they fear just how amazing they truly are!

Another little parasite I would like to shine the light on for your awareness to recognize, is the giving away of your own personal power, voluntarily. Yes, people do this and they do it often. We as humans are very powerful. We are the only living beings on this planet that can create the life we want right before our eyes, and obtain anything we set our minds to. Yet we constantly give away our personal power, thinking that other people are more deserving.

One of the most common practices I have seen locally is the giving away of one's own power to what people call spirit. This manifests in situations like this:

Meet Rick. He is in his mid-thirties and has been studying spirituality and loving, living in a spiritual community. He is a chef and wants his healing food to heal the lives of many people. He goes to the farmers market every Sunday and sells his food, and many people love it. He also has an aging father, and as time passes, his father needs more and more financial help. Yet, Rick isn't sure how to make more money, in fact he hates money. He thinks only the evil people of this world have it, and that we shouldn't even need it. He believes that love and prayer should sustain us, and we should all live by trade. When the budget surrounding his family gets tighter and tighter, Rick continues to think that spirit will provide, and that all he has to do is have faith, and lo and behold it must!

I walk up to Rick one day at the farmers market and ask, "how are things going?" He responds with a low tone, "I am stressed about money, and I need more to help my family." "Your food is very popular, why don't you expand and begin to create more tents at more farmers markets? Or even begin to market into grocery stores, or do live events?" I reply, thinking that he loves to make this food, and he would of course succeed, as people love it as well!

What was Rick's response you ask? "I have been praying to spirit, and she is guiding me to simplify my life. I don't seek more money, as I hate money. I think it controls people. I know spirit will provide, she is all around us."

I stood there amazed. As here was a very talented young man, sharing his gift with the people of this world, and they loved it. He was selling his gift for money, while simultaneously hating money, and also while being stressed about not having more money. Then stating that he hated money, and also giving his power away to spirit!

My jaw dropped. This is an example of how one can adopt what they think is a spiritual lifestyle. One that isn't interested in money, yet I'll share a little secret with you folks, money is what makes the world go round. Money is the symbolic energy of the exact reflection of what you are giving out into this world, and how many people you are touching and helping. If you're a millionaire, you must be helping millions of people with your gift. Why do you think actors get so much money? They literally entertain millions of people on a daily basis, and their energetic compensation reflects that very act.

By choosing to think that there is something greater than yourself, and choosing to give away your power to what you think created you, is shirking the very gifts that the creator gave you! Here is a quote that speaks to this line of thinking, "*God's gift to us is more talent and ability then we'll ever hope to use in this lifetime... Our gift to God is develop as much of that talent and ability as we can in this lifetime.*" The quote does not state that we give our power to God, it states that we take the power God gave us and we utilize it to the best of our ability!

If you choose to hate money, then money will not be attracted to you. It's the same as anything else in this world. Like attracts like, hate attracts hate.

One could speculate that Rick may be living in a deep seat of fear for how powerful he really is, instead of taking a step into the larger unknown of his reality. He is holding himself back by using phrases like "spirit will guide me." Or "spirit will provide." I answer to this, as this is an action step toward giving your power away, and saying these lines does not make you a spiritual person, it makes you a powerless human living in a world of delusion. You're choosing to give your power away. I offer up the alternate view of knowing this. Everything on this planet was given to us by spirit, but the beings that have what they have, is because they went for it, they developed their inner-strength and they cultivated themselves into warriors for what they believe in. They did not sit back and pray to spirit to care for them, they cared for themselves. They didn't see themselves at spirit's disposal, they saw themselves as an extension of spirit. Therefore, they had unlimited gifts and strength to obtain and grasp the true desire of their heart.

Are there disempowering statements you use to feed your inner-fears of who you truly are? Are you expecting others, or spirit to take care of you? Do you think just praying is an action step? Praying is a beautiful ground-work to lay out on a daily basis that can surround you with positivity, but it must be followed by action.

Let's always remember, praying is beautiful and it's planting the seed of what can come, however, one must water that seed with actual physical action steps in order to reap the harvest of the prayer planted. If not, one will reap sheer silence from spirit, or whatever external circumstance you think rules your life. When in fact, my dear, no one rules your world but yourself, and it's about time everyone on this plane takes their power back and begins to fulfill their destiny.

Another pattern that may be leaking your self empowerment is blame, which to me is thinking that circumstances in this life are happening *to* you, and life is not happening *for* you. Blame comes from the negative mindset that we don't create our own reality, that life happens to us and we can't do anything about it. It's that poor me attitude that throws the infant on the ground when she has a tantrum for not getting the ice cream she wanted! Or it's the 13 year-old teenage girl, who thinks her parents are ruining her life. This is a common practice as a child grows and develops, but I think many of us forgot to leave that negative pattern behind as we grew from children to adults, and instead of reclaiming our power, we continue to think we don't have any.

There is a natural cycle of blame that we experience as kids, because truth is, we are under the rule of older people and our freedom is limited in some regard, but as we turn 18 and are able to leave the nest and create our own life, we habituate this pattern instead of shedding it. Another, and a more substantial layer to blame, is thinking that all the bad things that happened to us in our life deserved to be put upon the shoulders of another person. Meaning, if we experienced abuse, we blame others for that said abuse, not even realizing that us having the ability to survive the abuse gave us more profound strength, more incredible insight on how we can truly help others. Without seeing this fact, we take a bad situation and keep it in the category of bad, but we can transform the situation by taking that blame from a negative action, to a positive one. Example:

> Cassie grew up with a father who was mostly drunk, spanked her and her brother, and never treated her mother kindly. She began to fear him and even hate him. She saw every action he did as horrible, and couldn't wait until she left the house and started her own life. When Cassie turned 18 she left home, got a job and began to date. She knew that she never wanted anyone else to experience the pain and suffering she did from being around someone who she thought was supposed to love her, so she made a silent promise to herself to never be a drunk, and to only treat others with love and kindness. Cassie soon met a sweet man who was the opposite of her father, which was in line with her deep-seated promise she made to herself. Cassie and her boyfriend traveled together, and loved one another for a couple of years, until they began to have children of their own. She still had much pain and anger towards her father, blaming him for her lost childhood and all the sorrow she had to endure. This blame caged her in a sense, from being free to see the beauty she had already created in her new life, and it always weighed on her in a subtle way. This pattern, always weighing on Cassie, will never quite allow her to experience the full joy of love around her, and will always weigh her down in a sense. So how can she release herself? When in fact, her father was not kind to her.

Truth is, Cassie's father played the role he was meant to play! He showed up in her life, treated her the only way he knew how to treat her, and through this training course Cassie became kind. She became compassionate, and also stopped the perpetuation of abuse when she began her new family. Her father taught her how to transmute pain into joy via self-commitment. He taught her how to take care of herself by staying sober, and how to love a man without abusing him. He taught her how to raise her kids with the kindness of a butterfly, and how to take care of her family with superhero strength. The only missing link in this whole wave of knowing, for Cassie, was taking the perspective that pain is a bad thing, when in fact pain was the very motivation that inspired Cassie to create a beautiful abundantly love-filled life. Her disapproval of her father, allowed her to bring another man into her life that was nothing like him, that served her highest good.

The weight that kept Cassie down, was the perspective that her father should have been different than who he truly was, and this act of non-acceptance caused her pain. Blaming him just for what she perceived as negative, and not blaming him for the positive outcome she created, was a misalignment, and allowed her to stay caged in pain around her father.

Accepting what is, and also seeing the positive outcome that comes from negative circumstances, is a superpower you can cultivate, for it's a chosen perspective you can take at any moment in your life, releasing yourself from the pain you hold so dear inside of yourself.

Also, always remember that there is no written law via God, that says we have to have two kind, amazing parents that always love us, and serve us, in order for us to grow up and become incredible people. In fact, it seems that the individuals that had the most abusive, sad childhoods have the ability to overcome this experience, and create the most strength, the most drive, and the most cultivated inner-power to truly create the life they want. For they have lived this very lesson, and their strength has been tested. Once your strength has been tested, you then have a knowing inside of your being that shows how strong you are, how capable you are, and how nothing can take you down. Nothing!

When people in my life "do me wrong" or blindside me, I say this to them, "thank you for showing me my true strength. Thank you for giving me a chance to test the depth of my compassion and understanding, and thank you for showing me what I don't want to be."

We are here to evolve our souls and whether you like it or not, evolution comes in many forms, and most of these forms are struggle, grief, the over-coming of fear, and circumstances that test or strength. So I say, "bring it on!" as my chief aim in life is not to roll over and submit at the first sign of bumps in the road, but to see these bumps as a training course for my soul, so I may cultivate myself into a state of awakening, and then help all those around me do the same.

PART II

"There are two basic motivating forces: Fear and Love.
When we are afraid, we pull back from life.
When we are in love, we open to all that life has to offer
with passion, excitement, and acceptance.
We need to learn to love ourselves first, in all our glory
and our imperfections. If we cannot love ourselves,
we cannot fully open to our ability to love others or our
potential to create. Evolution and all hopes for
a better world rest in the fearlessness and
open-hearted vision of people who embrace life."

John Lennon

CHAPTER SEVEN:

Giving our Power Away to Past Trauma

"The secret of success is learning how to use pain and pleasure instead of having pain and pleasure use you. If you do that, you're in control of your life. If you don't, life controls you."

~ Tony Robbins

In order for us to walk through this life fully-empowered in our being, we must take stock of the past, honestly looking into old traumas and events where we may have left pieces of our self, due to the fact that we have yet to move on or truly let go, allowing us to be all powerful in the here and now. There are many different life events we have all traversed through, and knowing that we have fully grasped the lesson from these empowering events is a great place to start when setting the intention of reclaiming one's power. Once we have reclaimed our power from past events and traumas, we will fully be standing in our own authenticity. We will be able to see things as they truly are in the present, rather than seeing them through the reflection of our past pain, and we will have the powerful ability to create the life we want to live.

This is a great time for me to take a moment and remind you that if you have undergone some extreme trauma or abuse, mere positive thinking cannot wish that trauma or pain away. One must authentically pull that trauma out by facing it, feeling the pain, and then releasing it with taking away the teachings that traumas and pain do offer us. One may need a therapist or psycho-emotional therapy to truly be supported through their current state of mind, and this is a beautiful thing. Tony Robbins speaks about this, stating that you can't just chant, "there is no weed, there is no weed, there is no weed!" while standing over your weed-filled internal garden. You must pull those weeds out first! What we can do is train our mind to perceive that trauma as something we can then use to help the rest of the world, and this is empowering oneself.

When we go through a trauma or life event that hurts our being, we have two choices on how we want to perceive that life lesson. When viewed from the positive perspective, that whatever is taking place currently is here to make us stronger, make us more evolved and teach us compassion, then we will walk through any event knowing that it's a blessing to have an opportunity to test our own strength. However, if we go through a trial in our life where we see it as happening to us, that we had no choice in the matter, and we hold on to the pain like it's the last outfit we have to wear, then we will remain stuck in a disempowered state, seeing everything in the present moment through the glasses of that particular past trauma.

When these traumas or events accumulate, as we get older and move through our years here on earth, they can begin to stack in our field and this is why we have triggers. This is why when something happens to us in the day-to-day life that annoys or activates our pain body, we react with feelings much larger than necessarily appropriate for the actual current circumstance. We are living from our pain body, as we have yet to truly take our power back from whatever painful memory we are bringing with us into the future.

No one can ever take our power. It's our lack of perspective and our choice to give our power away in any circumstance that then depletes our power in the present. I want you to meet Tim. He is a man of 38 years, living his day-to-day life hoping to meet the woman of his dreams and settle down and get married. However, Tim had a very intense and painful relationship with a woman eight years ago, where both he and her cheated on each other and they lost their ability to trust one another. Due to the inability to face this problem head on in the present moment, Tim took this pain of betrayal with him long after the relationship had ended. I am saying this all with a deep sense of sympathy, as to be cheated on when one is in love is not an easy pain to bear, but to give your power away and carry this pain with you for eight years after the event has ended, is a much larger pain to bear indeed.

Tim did his best to let it go. He saw a therapist and talked about it, but what he did on another level is make a silent promise to himself to protect his heart from feeling this pain in the future. He decided to build walls up around his heart, so when another woman were to enter his life he wouldn't just allow himself to jump into the relationship so foolhardy, he would "protect" himself.

Many of you may be thinking, well this sounds rational, yes? He had pain, he learned from the pain, and now he is implementing a strategy to help himself not feel pain in the future. However, we must take an honest note. Whenever we choose to not arrive fully with an open heart in any given situation, we are removing ourselves from the very thing our soul is seeking, love.

For we can't feel love, and be in love, if we are protecting our hearts. I am not suggesting one should lay their heart on the table at any sign of attraction to the next woman. What I am suggesting, is that if you're going to build walls around your heart as a remedy for a past pain, then you're not healed from the past pain, and you have yet to glimpse the strength you could have received from that event. Instead, Tim has chosen to live from his painful body, not his empowered body. This is a very big shift in perspective I am asking you to grasp here, for the mind can rationalize holding on to pain for years. But if this is the choice you're making, this choice can spoil any chances for riches, love, and health for you in the present or the future. It's a cosmic fact that if we carry the pain from the past and live from that place in the present, we have no ability to harness the empowerment and self-confidence it takes to truly attract what it is we want in this life. Read this sentence again, and allow it to serve as a motivating factor in your new found ability to switch your past perspectives from one of disempowerment, to one of self empowerment.

What is happening to Tim now, as he is 38 years old, eight years after his painful cheating relationship? Now he has decided to carry this pain with him, and yes he did make that decision. You see, many people think that if they deem the life event so painful, and so hurtful, that they are then given a pass to carry that pain with them into the future. Instead of just learning from the event, and fully moving on, Tim has decided to carry the pain into the future, and now it has been eight years of dating this girl and that girl, all for about three-month periods of time. He never really opens his heart to any of these new women, he just moves through the dating process, removed and guarded, making excuses that they aren't really what he is searching for. So that when they begin to fall for Tim, and ask for a deepening in their relationship, Tim then breaks off the relationship and moves back into his closed-off heart. Time and time again this happens, until one day Tim meets a woman who we will call Annie, whom he thinks actually carries the traits that he is looking for, so this relationship takes on a new tone.

This relationship goes on for seven months, a new record for Tim. However, in the relationship, Annie can feel the closed off sensation of dating a man that has been wounded, and is continuing to live from those wounds. She can inspire him to choose to open his heart, but the decision must come from Tim, to let go of his past, in order to even have the ability to see the beauty that lays in front of him, in the form of this new woman.

You see, if we are living from our past pain, then we don't even truly have access to what it is we are experiencing in the present. It's like we are wearing glasses, and the lenses of the glasses are filtered through past life events that color the beauty of the present. This way of being, drains our self-confidence as well as our ability to take our power back, because living from the past is living with the attitude that life is happening to us, and not for us. That we don't have control of what we are creating, rather than knowing we do have control and taking the steps to re-program our being with positive affirmations and propelling us into the life we want. No doubt this takes courage, and no doubt one must put in a daily commitment to make this happen. However, the rewards are so great that doing anything other then this seems like one is choosing to lose out on their own life.

With Tim's glimpses of insight into Annie being colored by his past pain, he keeps his heart blocked. She allows patience to enter into her actions in their relationship. As for her, she knows she can only truly give and receive love with an open heart, so Annie showed up into the relationship with Tim living in the present, open hearted and ready to learn about this new person giving everything she has to the relationship. Tim on the other hand, is living in his past pain, and allowing the wall in front of his heart to stay upright for the entire seven months of their dating relationship.

Seven months was all Annie could take of dating a man with a closed heart. When one heart is open, and the other closed, it feels like one is starving, sitting at the dinner table with their hands tied behind their back, while on a plate right in front of their eyes is an abundance of five-star cooked food just resting there. They have no ability to eat it, and the more they gaze at the plate, the hungrier and hungrier they become! It's torture as it's so close, all it would take is one small adjustment in order to be able to eat such a beautiful and satiable meal!

The metaphorical meal I am here referring to is love, so while Annie's patience has ended, she encourages Tim to open his heart to her and to begin to actually show up and participate fully in the relationship, for she realizes she is no longer happy with him. And unless he can meet her where she is, she knows it's over. With this new ultimatum on the plate for Tim, he feels the pull of his past pain, and decides that he isn't sure if he even loves Annie, so why even try? He ends the relationship, feeling confused, disconnected, and lost.

Annie on the one hand, showed up giving 110% effort the entire relationship. She entered in the present moment, opened her heart, took a risk of it being broken, but also took a risk of her love being received and returned. And that is a risk worth taking as far as Annie is concerned.

Tim on the other hand, is stuck in the mental chatter, implementing excuses that are allowing him to rationalize how his past pain is okay, and serves him to hang on to. He feels that his timeline and movement through finding his love, must move at a slow pace. He must not fully jump into anything, and he must not give himself fully, for then he will be hurt. If Annie can't wait for his heart to open, then she must not be the right woman for him. This may be true. However, is Tim really experiencing his life fully? Is he really opening up to what he truly wants? Or is he living through a series of excuses that keep him bound to his past pain?

All of these questions are only up to Tim to truly decide, but they are also here to spark questions for you to ask yourself if there is something or someone you want in your life, but you're not achieving that, whether it is in regards to love, a job, a health concern, or an amount of money you want to make. Are there parts of yourself stuck in the past living from that pain, and then taking the ability away from you to fully show up in the present?

If you are truly giving 110% effort into any and all endeavors you're currently living in, then I would say you have achieved the ability to learn from the past, and live in the present. If there are excuses that tie you, and keep you bound to your past pain, which then subsequently removes your ability to show up with 110% effort in the present, then this may be a good place for you to begin to take stock into what is holding you back, and what lesson you need to learn to truly release yourself from the past in order for you to fully live in the present.

Using an objective statement like having the ability to put in 110% effort, is allowing a scale to arise in your mind's eye. Once you have this scale in your mind, think of your current job. Are you giving 110% to your current job? If so, then reward yourself. Rejoice and congratulate yourself! Praise and positivity feeds more positive actions, so it's important to reward oneself for these significant achievements! If you're not, then what past event has taken you out of fully being able to live in the present? Are you holding onto excuses like Tim was? Are you using these excuses to keep you safe in your pain, afraid to take the next step into the future? What perspective shift can you take in order to release this pain from your life, to allow you to take your power back, grow your self-confidence and then manifest the life you truly want?

A perspective shift for Tim could resemble this... Tim's current perspective is to see the past cheating relationship as a lesson for him to always keep his heart guarded, to never let people get to close to him (especially women) and to stay more focused on making money, and his job, rather than giving his heart over to a fulfilling relationship. Many men do this, as it's easier for men to solely focus on their jobs, than on love. However, they miss the link that it's the love for a woman that inspires them to harness the motivation to create the life they truly want to live. Every great man that has ever succeeded in this world, was in fact inspired by the love they had for a woman. When a man is in love, it activates the very thing inside of him that gives him the push to create, to maintain and to nurture those around him. It activates his feminine side, which then allows him to harness both the masculine and feminine inside of his being, making him an unstoppable force to be reckoned with. If the man shuts down to love, he lives primarily from his masculinity, losing the ability to be inspired, to nurture, and then to perhaps indeed take over the world!

So for Tim to leave his painful past, and enter into an abundant future being able to love himself fully first, then any woman he chooses to love, he must first forgive himself for being in the past relationship that hurt him. He must forgive himself and the woman involved, then from a place of forgiveness and compassion he must then switch his focus to see the abundant lessons he can learn from this event. He can choose to learn that the pain one feels from being cheated on is in fact, quite unbearable. He can channel this pain into a positive attribute by thanking it for inspiring him to never cheat on another woman he is with again, and to choose to only be with a woman in the future that matches this sense of integrity. He can also choose to see his open heart as an act of bravery rather than stupidity. Currently, Tim is kicking himself for wearing his heart on his sleeve and allowing this woman to crush it, when in fact it takes an epic amount of bravery to be able to love another fully and be vulnerable. This slight change in perspective allows one to be empowered rather than disempowered. It changes Tim's reaction from "I'm dumb for giving my heart so freely, I better protect myself in the future," to "I am so brave for giving my heart to a woman, this bravery will not be conquered, in fact it will grow as I have survived this relationship, and I will indeed survive any other relationship that comes my way." This attitude allows Tim to attract more fruitful relationships, rather than stay blocked and removed from the possibility altogether. Do you see how the small tweaks in perspective release one from their painful past, and allow them to paint a new self empowered picture that will better serve them in the future? It allows Tim to see himself with love, to see himself as brave and beautiful, which then empowers him to live fully in the present. Whereas the past viewpoint, which led to him shutting down his heart, put him in his pain body, which lowered his self-esteem, took away his ability to open his heart in the present, and therefore set him on a course to never fully being able to obtain his wish of being able to marry, have children and settle down...

The beauty and inspiration of all this info? Tim can change his life any second he so chooses! He can choose to change his perspective in an instant! He can take his power back, drop the line of excuses holding him close to his pain body and see himself as a brave and beautiful man ready to give himself fully into every, and any idea he sets his mind too! This ripple effect will then vibrate out into all other endeavors in his life, making him more successful, more loving and contributing more to the planet.

It's time for you to take stock and see which places in your life are you living from your past pain? What new perspectives can you obtain to release yourself and empower yourself? Sometimes the pain is so deep, one needs help climbing to a place where seeing the light is even possible. In these instances I offer resources in the back of this book, as it's the basis of the sessions I facilitate for my clients as well. When one is going to an outside person like myself, or another facilitator, it allows one to get the perspective outside of the pain body. For the facilitator is not caught up in the same trauma, so they then have the ability to see what the client has yet to access, and they can give this insight to the client, allowing them to release themselves from the past.

Sometimes, the pain one has been carrying is so embedded into their mind that just a shift in perspective isn't enough to bump them out of their disempowered state, and that's when we bring in the tools to imprint the subconscious with this new found insight!

If we have gained a new perspective that we understand, but somehow it hasn't shifted us out of our pain body, we must make a commitment to impressing this new perspective into our mind, so it may drop into the subconscious and manifest itself as our new way of being. This can be done in the form of a goal-like statement we write down and read to ourselves on a daily basis, where it will transform from a fifth-dimensional insight, to an actual state of being. You see, when we repeat an affirmation in the present tense, and then apply this on a daily basis with feeling, like it has already manifested into our life, then we have just accessed a route to manifestation for our new way of being! For this process will imprint into the subconscious, and over time will begin to express itself as the new empowered us! Very exciting indeed to have such a profound key to permanent change don't you agree? Just so we are clear, this is a universal law that does indeed work. One does not need to spend five years in talk therapy to change their way of being. This is an old law that we chose to believe. The truth is which Tony Robbins states on a regular basis, "change happens in an instant!" It does not have to be hard, it does not have to take five years in therapy, it literally can happen in an instant. The sooner it is that you align yourself with this truth, the sooner it is that you'll begin to be able to see it for yourself, happening in your own life.

An example of something that Tim can repeat to his subconscious on a daily basis, is to leave his past behind and to arrive fully in his fruitful present would be this:

"I am so happy and grateful now that I give 110% of my effort into everything I do. I am so happy and grateful I am living with an open heart, giving myself fully to true love so that it may manifest in my life, and I am so happy and grateful now that I fully love and cherish myself, allowing me to fully love and cherish the woman in front of me."

This is an example of a counter to the inner-thoughts that Tim has prescribed himself to for the past eight years. In the past, his mental attitude sounded something like this, "I need to protect myself from pain in the future, therefore, I'll implement a timeline that resonates with my pain body, keeping me from ever really having to open my heart in the present. Therefore confirming the fact that I will indeed be hurt by a woman, as she will end up leaving me as my heart is closed, and no one wants to date a man with a closed heart. I will continue to carry this pain with me into the present moment as I see it as an excuse of a shield that will offer me protection in pain. However, it will also offer me protection from all other great things that will never truly be able to bear fruit, as I must be able to fully show up in every endeavor to reap my rewards. But I choose pain over abundance."

You can read the extreme difference in how these two affirmations make your body feel. For the first affirmation allows the body to open fully, which then leads to the ability to receive fully, which then allows one to be fully living their life. The second affirmation shuts down receptivity, takes away one's power to create and live in the present, and shuts one down from higher guidance as well, for one cannot compartmentalize the opening of one's heart.

Meaning, if you close your heart down from pain, you're also closing your heart down from receiving sixth sense insight, and feeling tuned into your inner truths.

I would go so far as to say that Tim not only feels disconnected from romantic love, but he has also shut down his antennae to being able to tune into higher guidance, and be drawn into his true meaning on this planet. For you can't keep part of your heart open to just insight, while the rest of it is closed to love. Hence, the example of being able to show up giving 110% effort in all areas of one's life. This is how one leads themselves to health and vitality, to riches, and to manifesting whatever it is they desire fully. I will get into the harnessing of the sixth sense in the next chapter. However, I truly want you to understand what is holding you back from being able to receive this sixth-sense insight first. When you decide to live from your pain, you're shutting down imperative channels that will fill you with guidance in the present. Whether this shutdown came from a past love lost, or trauma from your parents, or lack of nurturing for you by yourself, all of these areas need to be fully examined and then noticed to be able to change them.

Once you have taken stock in what is holding you back from truly being an empowered individual in the present moment, you'll have the ability to change your perspective on what happened, take your power back, and then harness an affirmation that implements this knowing in your subconscious mind that will then ripple out into a feeling in your body. That vibration will then attract the same vibration into your life, for this is the law of the universe and the sooner you fully absorb this concept, the sooner you will be able to obtain whatever it is your true heart desires. Before we move onto chapter eight, go over the process of reclaiming your power, and take honest stock of your life and how are you showing up and where you're holding yourself back.

1. Which areas of your life are you choosing to live from your pain body?

2. What excuses have you created to tell yourself which hold you in the past taking away your ability to live fully in the present?

3. What perspective shift can you take to release you from your past and allow you to live fully empowered in the present?

4. Do you need a facilitator to offer you a new perspective that may help you release yourself from the past?

5. What affirmation can you write down (now) that is in the present tense that would activate through feeling how you want to be now, and how you want your life to look like in the present moment?

6. Can you make a commitment to repeat this affirmation with feeling, twice daily until it has transformed into your way of being?

Once you have answered these questions earnestly, you'll have a heightened state of awareness to receive the next chapter on the sixth sense. But it is imperative that you understand in order to cultivate activating, and receiving information from the sixth sense, we must first be able to stand in our authenticity to be able to recognize the hits we get. If we are living in a disempowered state, then confusion is more abundant than clarity. And when confusion is more abundant, the deciphering of the sixth sense code may seem like more work than pleasure. Once the sixth sense is tapped into, you'll begin to be divinely guided to each moment every day, that will be the activation of the unfolding of whatever it is you wish to manifest in this life, and that I can promise you.

CHAPTER EIGHT:

Activating the Sixth Sense, the Magical Key to Endless Manifestation

"Gratitude is an attitude that hooks us up to our source of supply. And the more grateful you are, the closer you become to your maker, to the architect of the universe, to the spiritual core of your being. It's a phenomenal lesson."

~ Bob Proctor

Setting the stage for you to encompass the ability to tune into, activate and then manifest through the sixth sense of your system is my goal in this chapter, and I would like to begin by saying that everyone has a different relationship to that sense in their own lives. So as I explain this quality, I am going to give examples with the intention that it raises your awareness so you begin to sense what this means for you, not what this looks like for others. For it's your very own relationship to yourself, that allows you to tune into this form of higher guidance. Once you do, you'll have the key to manifest anything and everything it is you want in this life. For the sixth sense is the cosmic tie to all that is, and all that ever will be in the here and now... nothing is out of reach!

Your human body is like a tuning fork. It's made of vibrations that you create with your mind, along with cellular karmic structures that circulate your system at a speed that words don't even have the ability to describe. The goal of finding your own recipe for hearing, feeling, and utilizing your sixth sense will give you the ability to see the plan, and steps it takes to create that state of health, or manifest whatever it is you're working towards in this life. So how can you hear or feel what is coming through for you if you're disconnected from your body or tuning fork? Well... you can't!

In the previous chapter, I told a story in reference to Tim, and how he had chosen to live in the present moment in pain, carrying a trauma from his past with him, which disconnected him from his heart as well as his insight. In reference to this particular story, Tim's ability to be present with his sixth sense is clouded by his current pain or trauma, and that pain overrides the antennae that reach up to the infinite. So what does Tim do? How can he release himself from his pain?

First he must make a decision that he wants to be tuned into something greater, and he wants to let go of his past and live whole-heartedly in the present. Once he has made this decision, he will then have the opportunity to work through his issues. With every corner he turns in this healing process, he realizes he is getting closer and closer to his true authentic self, and as he is getting closer and closer to his true authentic self, he is in turn getting more and more able to tune into what's greater, and what's available to him in the here and now.

A metaphorical example of this energetic layout looks like this. Let's say you just bought a radio. It's all in one piece and it's super shiny and has a great ability to be receptive to many stations, you can listen to rock, jazz and even some booty shaking hip hop. It's quite incredible! As you begin to enjoy this radio, you take it with you everywhere you go, showing it to your friends and family, and as this radio begins to traverse the world, it gets bumped into walls, creating scratches, you drop it a couple of times chipping off pieces and corners, and then one day you have a big accident. Dropping the radio down from a one-story building, the radio splits into four different pieces, shredding itself on the concrete. You never meant to drop the radio, in fact you loved it with you whole heart!

You miss being able to listen to all those stations and hear all the music you loved so dearly, so you try to piece the radio back together again with some duct tape and zip ties. It plays, but now it only gets one station and it's NPR, which does NOT allow you to dance and play. Instead, it dampens your dance moves, and makes you mostly frustrated! So instead of carrying your radio around with you, you lose interest, put it in the top of your closet, and begin to seek entertainment elsewhere. You can remember the fulfillment you had when you had access to all those stations, but the fact that the radio is so broken puts you in a state of helplessness. Instead of finding a specialist to fix it, you cave into a state of non-action, and stop trying.

This is what most people in this world do when they lose touch with access to higher insight. They allow the circumstances of their lives to determine their state, rather than taking back the power that they were given at birth, to access any station they so desire, and put the time and energy into healing themselves, and then have access to any station they want at any time. Yes it takes work, yes it MAY take time, it may not take time, but it does take EFFORT. It seems that when it comes to helping oneself, and stepping out of one's pain these days is something most people are shying away from. Rather than stepping up to bat at the game of their life, they prefer to sit on the sidelines, not taking any risks, but also not getting to experience any glory if the team wins!

Once you make the choice, you already take your power back. You see that there is a road to eternal happiness and fulfillment, and you set your focus at obtaining it. And I have a promise for you, if you set your scope to fixing yourself (which is saying that you're not even broken – when I say fixing yourself, I mean that you raise your awareness to the knowing that you're not broken, then your system matches this sense of empowerment, and that's when the being becomes whole once more.) Then, you have just stepped into the motion of walking towards your destiny and having access to the path that is going to get you there.

So now you have made the choice. You know that there are people out there to help you fix your radio, and you also know that your effort and commitment to this process will only lead you to winning the healing battle, and you graciously accept the challenge. As you walk this path you obtain different insight from different healers, raising your awareness to the fact that you're perfect, you're powerful, you're whole and you manifest your own reality. Now your tuning fork is activated, and now you have the ability to access the insight that will unfold the path before your eyes, allowing you to have the life you truly desire!

I myself have many different recipes for how I receive insight from higher guidance, and it starts with caring for myself and loving my system. Or another way of saying this, is that I actively keep my tuning fork tuned in. I create structure in my life that supports my growth on a daily basis, I have rituals that soothe my nerves and support my mind, and I practice self-care in a loving way, supporting the very thing that brings in the awareness.

I begin every morning with my gratitude book, which is a book where I record the ten things I am grateful for, writing them in the present tense whether they are things I already have or things I want to manifest. As I write them, I feel them as if it was happening in the present moment, and I see in my mind's eye myself already obtaining what it is I am writing about. This practice not only tunes your physical system into a vibration of positivity, which is a powerful amplifier for the higher wisdom, but it strengthens my ability to imagine, feel, and practice faith which are the very three ingredients needed to be able to obtain insight from a higher place in time. You see, these rituals, if you view them from a one dimensional perspective, can be diminished to seeing it as someone just writing fairytale things down in a book, and then going about their day.

If you tune into your sixth sense, you'll notice while you are practicing this morning's gratitude journal, that you're actually changing the cells of your body to a vibration of positivity. This then opens your heart, which then opens your entire field, and once your system is submerged in this positive state of empowerment, you then notice that you're writing the very things that you want in your life in the present tense. What is this doing? It's showing you, and giving you, a daily practice of empowering yourself. It's showing you what it looks like, and feels like to be the power of one's own destiny. It shows you how to take your power back and really obtain what it is you want.

If you're in a state of poor physical health, and you have been seeing this doctor and that doctor, you continue to decline, and all you can focus on is your pains, and your illness, then you'll feel helpless, like you don't have a way out. Your focus is on what is not working rather than what is working, but you have a choice, always!

You can choose to take back your destiny, and begin a gratitude journal practice. Your journal may look like this, and as your writing this in the morning before you leave your bed, you're also feeling what it feels like to already have these statements obtained in your life. If that's initially a struggle for you, then you activate another superpower you have that's called compassion. You give yourself time while you practice activating and channeling your emotions in the way you want them to go. This may take time, or it may happen right away, but for goodness sake, begin to have compassion for your beautiful self.

1. I am so happy and grateful now that my body is in a state of vital health.
2. I am so happy and grateful now that I am fully empowered and have the ability to take my power back and control the destiny of my health!
3. I am so happy and grateful now that I nurture myself with nourishing foods.
4. I am so happy and grateful now that I have trained my mind to see the positive and have truly begun to create the life I want for myself!
5. I am so happy and grateful to be surrounded by a loving and nourishing community.

6. I am so happy and grateful now that I see my current health challenge as an opportunity for growth!

7. I am so happy and grateful now that I have the ability to help others through their own pain and struggle!

8. I am so happy and grateful to be a source of inspiration for myself and others.

9. I am so happy and grateful now that I have $50,000 in my savings account!

10. I am so happy and grateful now that my heart is overflowing, and I fully understand I am the creator of my own destiny!

This is what a daily gratitude may look like, and while you're writing each line, you're focusing on what it feels like to have already obtained what it is you're writing about, and allow those feelings to flow through your whole system. Over time, this simple yet powerful practice embeds your life with positive energy. Once your system is awakened to what's positive, your heart opens to possibilities and that opens your ability to see, hear, and feel insight from higher planes.

Your heart must be open to receive, for if it's closed, you're closing yourself off from the very thing that created you in the first place. This closure will dis-empower you from your God-given right of creating your own destiny.

Once I have done my morning gratitude journaling, I then do my morning transcendental meditation practice, which is me sitting for twenty-minutes focusing on the mantra my teacher gave me. TM allows my body to unwind, my heart to open, and a calm wave to flush my system. It's a practice I do twice daily, and it stills my system from stress, allowing everything to unwind.

As life continues to get more and more fast, with all the technology and systems popping up all around us, we are constantly feeling the push to move faster, to accomplish more. We want a ten-minute oil change, not a one-hour oil change. We want to lose weight in a week, not a year! We want to be able to work ten hours a day and not have to eat, rather than nourish ourselves and realize that once we commit to nourishing ourselves, we actually begin to accomplish more. There is a saying which I love, "Slow down to go further."

This statement is the symbol of TM for me, as it slows me down, and allows me the space in my reality to make choices. I can choose to stop working and eat a healthy meal, I can choose to go for my goals and accomplish more, without the frantic energy of rushing and hurrying to accomplish all that I have set in front of me.

Things in my life don't necessarily change from TM, but my relationship to what happens in my life has changed from my TM practice, and this is the most priceless gift I have ever given to myself. I am no longer reactive, rather now I am responsive. I choose how I want to respond and have complete control over my emotional state, which is something I was lacking before I practiced TM.

Another magical component of this practice is that I receive massive downloads while I am trying to focus on my mantra in meditation. I actually begin to get flushed with the very insight that helps me tune into what I have to do next in whatever project I am currently working on. So if I am working on writing another book, or I am stuck on what to put into my next chapter, I begin my TM practice, and like a flash in my mind I see the answer. I feel a truth of resonance in my body, and I immediately see the next step of action I must take to accomplish what it is I'm working on. This is a perfect example of "slow down to go further." For by choosing to slow down, sit in silence for twenty minutes, twice a day, I am amplifying my ability to receive insight. I then trust and honor that insight, as it resonates as a truth in my body. Once I finish my meditation, I write down all that I received, and I then set those insights into motion immediately.

This is one of my unique ways I receive insight. Another is by asking open-ended questions out loud. This example is something I learned to do from Doctor Richard Bartlett, a man who brought a practice called Matrix Energetics into this world. By asking open-ended questions, we activate the right side of the brain. Open-ended questions cannot be answered by the left side of the brain, for an open-ended question can not be rationalized. Once the left side shuts down, the right side opens, and the right side is directly connected to your heart field, which is the strongest and most vibrant field of your entire system. It radiates up to twenty-feet outside your body. That's quite a large and expansive tuning fork, if you ask me! So you have just asked an open-ended question, your left brain gives it to the right side, the right side drops this information into your heart, and bam! The heart then shoots this question out into the universe.

Scientifically speaking, you just intentionally set your vibration to match the curiosity of your question, then projected it out from your heart field into the universe. The universe then resonates with these questions, and shoots back the answer to this question. This does work. One must keep an open mind during this process, and a childlike playful attitude, for most times the human mind is so closed to the actual magic we have access to, that sometimes we miss the answer, because we are either consciously or unconsciously looking for what we think the answer should be, thereby missing the actual insight. But if we set our tune or vibration to staying open, then we will have the ability to receive the answer, and most times the answer is so incredible, so inspiring that it can often change the very course of one's life.

Earlier this year I was at a crossroads, I wanted to step out of the current business I was running, and wanted to find a way to help, serve, and raise the awareness of more people in this world. I also wanted to raise my income, and I wanted to love what I was doing on a daily basis, learning, growing, and serving, while being compensated with an abundance unlike anything I had ever seen before.

I asked an open-ended question, "what would my next entrepreneurial adventure look like, where I am serving millions of people, creating something that helps people with pain and understanding of their bodies and minds, and brings in a financial abundance matching the amount of people I am serving, which will be millions?"

I asked this question on a Monday, and on Tuesday morning I woke up and got a full inspirational idea to start a company that made medicinal tinctures, pain salves, and oils that would help millions of people! I began to see the marketing capabilities, and I also began to feel in my entire body that this was one of my callings, this was a gift I had been given in this life, to work with herbal remedies, and it was time to express that gift into the world. On that day, I started to buy different herbs in bulk, I began to research the branding idea I wanted to use, and I began to see the company form in my mind's eye. I saw how I could structure the company to provide an entirely different work environment for my employees. I would give them yoga, and massages, and scholarships to workshops that would allow them to awaken to their own highest potential. And I saw this as a platform to begin my journey of serving millions of people on this planet.

I chose to not question this insight, but to move forward creating weekly goals, with one large end goal, and this is how White Fox Medicinals™ was birthed into this world!

Many people are actually very able to succeed in receiving the insight, but once they do, they then allow their negative paradigms or old life patterns to start with negative self-talk. Then the negative self-talk closes the heart, allows the shoulders to curl, and takes away our own inner-power. We begin to listen to the negativity in our head, and we discourage ourselves, coming from a place of fear rather than a place of love. So how do we stop this self-sabotage? Really it's quite simple, for once you know in your very own awareness that all it is, is self sabotage. When it arises in your life, you see it as such, and when you see it for what it is, which is just fear arising in the form of negativity, then that very awareness creates the space in your field to choose to leave it behind, or to feed it further. Once you make the choice over and over again to leave it behind, and to choose to focus your awareness on what it is you DO want to create, that will grow in strength and your inner-negativity will loose it's power over you.

You're currently making the decisions to change your whole life, so take the daily necessary steps to doing this on a daily basis, and over time you'll grow in positivity, faith, and trust. And the negativity, doubt, and fear will diminish, freeing you into birthing yourself into the being you want to be!

An old story showing how this truth manifests in your life…

At the edge of a fire pit sat an old grandfather and his grandson. As they tended the flames and enjoyed one another's company, the grandson looked up at his grandfather and asked, "grand-father, how come I keep getting upset at myself and my brother? How can I have a happier life like you?" The Grandfather smiled as the wrinkles on his face danced, and he spoke in a very soft, yet powerful tone as he shared this old world story with his grandson. "Well my son, in every person there lives two wolves, and these two wolves are both very, very powerful,and are always very, very hungry. The more you feed one or the other, the more that wolf grows. One wolf is positivity, faith, love, trust, happiness, devotion to others and self, and playful. The other wolf is fear, betrayal, jealousy, hatred, greed and self-centeredness. If you feed the wolves they will grow. However, if you make the choice right now to just feed one wolf over and over again, it will get stronger. It will grow more and more prominent inside of your body, while the other wolf will eventually starve, weaken, and die off entirely. That is how powerful you are my grandson. Now which wolf will you decide to feed?"

This story has always stuck with me, for it's a daily choice to feed whichever wolf it is that you want to grow, and it's your choice to starve the wolf inside of you that you want to die. But first you must make a decision, then you must actually take action on that decision. It takes commitment, drive, and a daily choice to work on this. Once you do, your entire life can change in one instant, and when you begin to get your daily insights from the higher power, you'll have the fuel and drive to back that insight and ride the wolf of positivity and love into manifesting your heart's desire.

So I ask you now, dear ones… what wolf do you choose to feed on a daily basis? How much is this life on earth worth to you, and what do you want to do while you're here?

I set a concrete goal years and years ago, that this life I have, will mean something to millions of people long after I die. That my effort, which I give forth on a daily basis will heal, shift, raise awareness, and bring joy, peace and happiness onto this planet. That my legacy of effort will live on long after I pass, and always serve to awaken, uplift, and inspire all those I touch on a daily basis. This goal led me to strive to get to know myself better. To change, evolve, and raise my own awareness with the inner-trust that once I do this, the rest will unfold.

I commit to trusting. I commit to living and feeling unconditional love, and I commit to praying that you have the strength, willingness, and inspiration to then do that for yourself. For once we all wake up and put in the effort, the world we can create is the very world we wish our children to have the opportunity to live in. A world where love and honoring comes first. A world where the awakened ones lift everything around them to new heights of understanding, and we leave pain behind us. We have abolished the negative wolf, and as a whole we feed the wolf of love and positivity. We are all in this together, and it's time we started acting on this knowing. There is no separation between yourself and myself. What I do to myself I also do to you, and what I do to you I also do to myself. Walking through this world with this level of awareness, allows nothing but love to be passed around. For we can no longer take advantage of others when we see no separation between them and us, we see only wholeness everywhere we look.

I would like to end this chapter with offering you this statement for your morning gratitude practice:

I am so happy and grateful now that I choose love, and see all those around me as connected to myself. So I walk with generosity, I walk with an open heart, and I serve all those around me as I am serving God. For I know this is the same as serving myself, for there is no separation between beings in reality, separation is only in the mind.

CHAPTER NINE:

Riding the Wolf of Positivity, Leave the Masses to Brighten Your Spark

"What you seek is seeking you."

~ Rumi

The intention of this chapter will be to outline the alchemical properties that make up a positive attitude, while simultaneously activating your own self-confidence in order to express yourself fully, which most times means you'll be standing alone and away from the masses. Much of what I am about to say will resonate at a soul level, for it's the yearning every soul feels once we go from being a child, expressing our self fully, to that first instance where we were made fun of, or put down for being ourselves, possibly crushing the light that is seeking to shine even brighter, now that we are adults.

I am in no way stating that the masses are "negative," and you standing alone is "positive" for there is no judgment here. I just want to light a fire under your butt, to find the strength to truly go for what it is you dream of, not allowing external input to guide the internal destiny you know you're here to commence.

For many painful years I myself tried to fit in with the herd, and while I was trying this painful act, I felt a deep structure harden over my heart. I gave my power away to the masses, allowing them to decide who I should be, and what I should do with my life. It was so painful, that in my early twenties I said no more, and put every ounce of energy I had to developing my self-confidence and reclaiming my power back.

It was confusing for me to see so many people around me doing what others around them were doing, ignoring their own inner voice that was calling them to their own gift. Whether it was fear, or confusion holding them back, I knew that everyone around me had a beautiful gift locked up inside of them, but that we all had to learn how to cultivate the strength to step outside of what we thought others would think, and go for that which we truly desire. To add to this confusion, when we begin to grow and change, we can activate the pain inside of others that they harbor for themselves, for not following their own truth. They can then project onto us, trying to keep us from evolving in order to not have to look at their own inner-pain and struggle. We humans are complex beings, but in that very same breath, it is also quite simple to make a promise to ourselves to always be authentic, strive for something greater, and do something profound with our lives. As it all starts with a desire, then take action on that very desire, and your entire life will begin to change before your eyes.

Before we get started, I would like to examine the vibrations of self empowerment compared to self-confidence, for the two may seem interchangeable. However, the difference of feel in the body when they are sufficiently obtained, is slightly different. And honing in on these symbolic words while walking out of what holds you back, can be a great first tool in your alchemical formula to creating the life you desire.

Self empowerment is the ability to cultivate the awareness that you are indeed a powerful being. You not only know this fact, but you're aware of this fact. You have the awareness in all circumstances in your life of how your interaction with circumstances can either activate you to give your power away to the person or circumstance, or you can maintain your self empowerment status and tune into your own heart and authenticity in any given moment. A self empowered individual knows they are God's form of highest creation. They know they have the right on this planet to always follow their heart, and for no reason will they ever give their power away to a circumstance, or another person. For they live from the place of faith and not fear. They live from a place of raised awareness, and not clouded by the masses of thought. They generate their own reality, based on their soul purpose, rather than following the herd to a mediocre life full of confusion, lack of ambition, and bowing to what may not be serving them or other beings on this planet.

Self-confidence on the other hand, is believing in oneself through the knowing that resonates in their awareness that they are whole unto themselves, they are beautiful inside and out, and they are here to learn the lessons one needs to learn to evolve, while maintaining a softness for oneself, loving oneself fully, and expressing that love and compassion at every turn of events that life throws their way. If a person is self confident, another person can cut them down, and the words will wash over them like water off of a duck's back. If a person is self-confident, they love themselves fully, with a vibration of compassion allowing any trial and tribulation to evolve the soul, rather than deplete, discourage, or dampen the soul.

Now that we have these two definitions, we can enter the same page and fully get the most out of the insight in this chapter. Let's start this insight with asking ourselves the following questions, really taking stock of where we are at this moment in time. So as the insight unfolds we can register where we need to apply, and what action we must take. Start to answer these questions from the core of your heart, and encompass yourself with a feeling of compassion while you do some real soul searching. The more you take stock in who you are, and where you are now, the better the road map for creating a new way of being for the future. I do encourage you to write your answers out on a separate sheet of paper, so as we move through the chapter, you can refer back to your current thought status, and also watch as you obtain insight from the chapter on how you can adjust the way you feel and see yourself, in an instant. For change doesn't have to be long and arduous, it actually happens in a second! I ask you to consider this as you move through the following paragraphs, allowing your soul to evolve and become empowered in a moments notice! For these words are set up to activate that knowing through resonance, as it already is a part of your being. You just have to resonate, then activate!

1. Do you feel like you are a self-confident person?

2. Do you move through life's situations honoring your own needs? Or do you tend to fold to the needs of others in order to live under the radar?

3. Do you speak your truth to those around you when you feel like you're not being honored or treated with kindness? Or do you keep your mouth closed in order to keep the peace or not cause any disturbances?

4. Do you consider your needs to be a disturbance to others?

5. Do you feel like you're following your soul's destiny? Or do you feel like you're following the masses because you're not sure what your soul's destiny even looks like?

6. When you think of yourself, do you feel a sense of positivity or a sense of negativity? Or maybe you feel a sense of neutrality?

7. Is there anyone currently in your life that doesn't support you and honor your needs?

8. Is there anyone currently in your life that always supports you and your chosen direction no matter what?

9. Is there a public figure, superhero, or person in your life you see as a self-confident, self empowered person that you want to emulate?

Beginning with question one. Do you feel like you're a self-confident person? Taking note of how you answered this question, or if you feel a sense of confusion around even how to answer due to unsure feelings, when you read the question does it resonate? Do you expand and feel a sense of gratitude or do you contract and feel a sense of negativity? I find that being a self-confident individual is directly linked to one's ability to be vulnerable. For the ability to be vulnerable is the most self-empowering action anyone can take in this world. It means you have the ability to put yourself out there. You have an idea, and you go for it not caring what others think or how others will respond. For that shows that your focus is outwardly driven. If your focus is inwardly driven, you're self-confident, you're able to put the needs of your soul as a first and foremost goal, and allow yourself to take action at all costs to give your soul a platform to shine! What a gift this is to the world!

I do believe many of us are highly aware of what vulnerability does to other people when it's viewed in action. For when one person is truly vulnerable, putting themselves out there for the world to see, an expansion happens to those viewing this process. A relaxation, as well as an invitation for them to do the same is activated, and through this action, we inspire unconditional love to pour into us while we share ourselves with the world. For there is nothing more touching to watch, than someone bearing their soul to the world. This can be noticed through the dating process much of the time…

When we first begin to date someone, we tend to try to be perfect. We don't fart in front of the other person, we certainly don't poo in front of them, and we most definitely always wear our best clothes and perform our best grooming. We never overeat in front of them, we always try to smell incredible, and we puff ourselves up a bit. It's sweet really, as both people get to know one another, the façade of being a perfect person begins to diminish, and the "real" you begins to make a debut. As this transition happens, moments of vulnerability tend to happen as well, for a romantic relationship tends to be the most intimate, body, mind and soul.

Meet Rob and Cindy. They have been dating for a month, and Rob wants to take Cindy dancing. They are both very much feeling one another, and very excited to be with each other, but Cindy is afraid that if Rob sees her dancing, then he will never want to see her again after that. To not be a sour puss, she decides to go out with him anyway, and maybe implement the hope that she can curtail having to dance. In her head, she makes up many excuses she can possibly share with him, like, "I'll tell him I just randomly twisted my ankle," or "I'll tell him the dinner upset my stomach and I just need to rest."

All her inner-plotting didn't have her prepared for what was really in store for the moment that deepened their entire relationship. Rob and Cindy had a beautiful dinner, and after Rob went to grab Cindy's hand in a hurry, as his favorite song came on, inspiring him to shake it! He got up from his chair so fast, and the music was already quite loud, which didn't leave Cindy any time to present her excuses to him, nor to try to pull away. So in a pure state of fear, she joined Rob on the dance floor, feeling stiffer than a stuffed scarecrow.

As she watched Rob start to dance, she noticed he didn't move to the beat at all. In fact, he almost looked ridiculous, and she couldn't tell if he was joking or really trying to dance. As her jaw dropped she realized, if he had the guts to dance like this in front of her, then certainly she had the nerve to allow him the same pleasure of seeing her expose herself as well. As the two began to cut a rug, they both laughed at their strange physical jerks they called dancing, and danced for the next three hours until they fell into one another's arms, feeling that peace that washes over us when we know we just walked through fear, and came out on the other end better for having done so!

Being vulnerable is an incredible act of bravery. It tells the world and your own soul that you're here to live this life to the fullest, and you're not ashamed of what God gave you! Which, my dear, one can transition into a powerful affirmation… I am so happy and grateful that I am living each moment to the fullest, and I am not holding myself back in any way. For I truly know, I am God's highest creation, and everything I have been given is a gift!

The true sadness is hiding these gifts, or hiding parts of ourselves from the world, due to fear or because we had made a silent promise to ourselves when we were five years old, after we were made fun of by Bobby on the playground for being strange. Then, from that moment on we chose to not be ourselves, because how awful it must be to be strange. We must fit in, for that will lead to more pleasure and less pain! Children are amazing and powerful, yet they are not equipped to fully understand the pain and pleasure connections we make, and how often, when we experience pain as a child. It's meant to be a platform for growth, not a platform for restriction. We have the choice to empower ourselves in the here and now as an adult, to free ourselves from whatever pain we endured in the past that is now making decisions for us in the present, and holding us back from truly experiencing our life. Choose vulnerability over fear, choose to empower yourself rather than give your power to the masses of thought. For the masses of thought are generally basked in pain, and why would you want to make a decision that doesn't lead to true happiness?

There are many injustices happening in this world today, which we can choose to see as opportunities, to fully speak our own inner-truth and show the world how one simple act of standing up for what is right, can indeed start a motion that then changes the world. If we were here to be lemmings and to follow the leader, then we wouldn't have been given all this consciousness. I see this in the image of a person standing before God, and God says to the man, "Son, I have given you power. More power than any other creature on the planet. I have also given you insight, so you may feel when it's time to use that power. I have also given you magic so you may change the world right before your very eyes, and I have also given you the ability to love, so that you may create a more beautiful world than one that I could have even imagined." The man stands there, sees all of these gifts that God has bestowed upon him, and then says, "thanks for all these gifts God! I think I'm going to see what that guy is doing over there instead of using these gifts, because it really seems like he already figured it all out." To which God replies, "That is an expression of the greatest gift I have given you my son, you also have the power to choose."

So choose! If there is a circumstance around you happening, and you don't speak up for your own rights and inject your own truth, you're giving all of your gifts away to someone who you have deemed more powerful than you, and I am here to tell you now my dear, no one is more powerful than you. We have all been given the same gifts, and most people choose to not honor any of them, or only choose to honor some. But the person who sets their mind towards honoring all of God's gifts, and spends his days improving himself and growing in awareness, will then have the ability, strength, and cultivated knowing that he then CAN create the life he wants to live. Once he does this, he also creates a ripple for the world to feel, that then inspires others to do the same. That's the power of vulnerability, and the power of following one's true soul purpose. It changes the world! I encourage you from a place of unconditional love and compassion, to begin asserting yourself where you feel injustice happening to you.

Meet Sandy. She has been working the same job for a couple of years and it isn't her favorite job, but it does pay her bills and allows her to generate a savings until she can figure out what she really wants to do with her life. One of the jobs that she performs happens to be for a friend of the family, and he has always paid her and other workers two-hundred dollars for the completion of each task he assigns. As she arrives at the job site, he explains to her that the industry is changing, and she is now going to receive one-hundred and seventy-five dollars for each task she completes. Feeling a sense of sadness grow inside of her, she walks into the workroom where morale is quite low and begins her work. The other employees get to talking about the drop in pay, and many commit to not returning to the job once they finish the current assignment. They begin to talk, and as it turns out, it's not industry standard, as many other jobs in the same field are still paying the full two-hundred, and when she realizes this, she also realizes that her employer is trying to save a couple hundred dollars for himself, rather than giving it to the people allowing him to run his business in an efficient and safe manner. Along with this realization, she also realizes that her employer is still making the same income, for nothing has fundamentally changed in his income. Yet, he has chosen to drop the income of his employees, so he can make a couple of extra hundred dollars.

Unfortunately, this is something that goes on in many businesses. The pay gap increases, and the business owners on top are so far removed from what their employees are experiencing, they make decisions based on falsified numbers out of greed, rather than honoring each individual as a person that's helping them run their business, and honoring them appropriately for such actions. We also know that some huge CEO's see this as an injustice, and do everything they can to always honor their employees, take care of their needs as they would their very own, and see this as the backbone of their company. To this insight, their company will always be a success. The business owners that chose greed over honoring, will eventually sink.

Sandy chooses to not say anything, increasingly feeling taken advantage of, and develops a sour taste in her mouth for her employer, making a silent promise to never work for him again. Another option for Sandy would be to see this situation as one where she can express herself in a kind, and loving way (vulnerability) and give her employer an opportunity to grow (compassion) while simultaneously taking her power back, and refusing to do any jobs that pay less than what she deserves (taking action for her own soul and not going with the masses).

There are opportunities for growth all around us. All we need to do is see them, go for them, and realize that, by us choosing to speak our truth, we are also helping those around us to see themselves in a deeper, more profound sense. If no one says anything to this employer who is cutting paychecks, he is not given the opportunity to see how his actions are affecting the people supporting his business, which may allow him to never change.

If you are reading this and thinking, how can I even follow what my soul wants if I don't even know what that is? I say to you, don't worry, as the perfect place to start to awaken this knowing is to begin by getting to know yourself, and beginning to evolve as a person. By committing to improving yourself on a daily basis, you're choosing to activate self-love, you're choosing to express to the world that you are committed to improving who you are, and you are ready for this journey of self-discovery. Once you make this commitment, set into motion an action plan of how you're going to do this.

Whether you decide to begin on your own, or to take a workshop in healing oneself, taking action in this arena every single day is crucial. You yourself know what you can commit to, and you want to make sure the goal isn't so far fetched that you'll fall short, which in turn will only add to your negative sense of self with the vibration of failing. You want to set yourself up for success by tuning into reality, seeing what you can accomplish every day, then rewarding yourself for completing that goal. Through this transition of setting goals, accomplishing them, and then moving forward, you are choosing to add to your self-confidence meter rather than detract from it.

I once knew a fine man. One who had aspirations bigger than the moon to change and evolve himself. His drive was intoxicating and inspiring, but this man lacked self-confidence. Every week he would set goals that derived from his enthusiasm, but were also quite unreachable on a consistent basis. He would be able to accomplish his goals for a week or two, then he would fall back into his old paradigms, feeling a sense of failure, as once again he couldn't complete his goals on a consistent basis. He would mope and feel sorry for himself, adding to his lack of self-confidence for a week or so, until he got a wave of inspiration that hit him again! And off to the races, like a time-old pattern, he would once again set lofty unreachable goals, try hard for a week or two or three, and once again, slip back into his old paradigm.

What this yo-yo expression does, is slowly chip away at one's self-confidence rather than slowly build one's self-confidence, and our goal is the latter. So create a goal, start as small as you wish, but large enough to have an emotional driving impact, then once you accomplish your goal, REWARD yourself! It's this act of rewarding and honoring your accomplishments, which then fuels your positivity, and also feeds your self-confidence. Once your self-confidence basket is full you'll have no issues being a self empowered human on this planet! A sample goal could be you're going to do your positive affirmations every morning, and every night for one week. After that week, you REWARD yourself and add one more piece to the self-improvement regime, maybe in the form of reading a paragraph from an inspiring book once daily, and so on. Having compassion through this process is crucial, as you're making a choice to break yourself away from old patterns, and create new ones that better serve you. Be kind, be patient, and talk to yourself from the inside out using only positive words, with the goal to completely eliminate any and all negative self-talk.

This leads us to raising our awareness around how we are treating ourselves, and how we are speaking to ourselves. For this may be the most important takeaway from this entire book. You must watch how you think, and you must only think in a positive manner. If this was your one goal in life, I do believe it would be the lifeboat that would then unfold whatever it is you truly want in your life! Most days, many of us don't even realize we are thinking, for we just let our thoughts go round and round, and we have a huge lack of awareness as to whether they are even positive or negative thoughts.

If we have cultivated the awareness that they are negative, we do nothing to change them from positive to negative, and this is a grave betrayal of the gifts God gave us. Our thoughts are indeed creating our reality, and if we are always putting ourselves down, always lowering our standards, and always seeing ourselves as low on the life totem pole, guess what our life is going to look like? Negative. If we make the conscious choice to watch our thoughts, see how we speak to ourselves, and we make an effort to counteract every negative thought with a positive thought, we will be alchemizing the very thing that has kept us down our entire lives. We will be choosing to turn lead (negativity) into gold (positivity). This is alchemy. It's the empowerment of self, to transition one element into an entirely new element that better serves us. Choose to be the alchemist of your own mind. Choose to take every negative thought, and transition it into a powerful thought! This powerful act, even if this is all you do, will indeed change your whole life. That I can promise.

For it is a universal law, that whatever the mind thinks, it manifests, and whatever you choose to think with emotions, behind that it imprints the subconscious mind, which then creates a vibration in the body. And that very vibration then draws in that same resonance from the outside world. You want more opportunities? Cultivate them in your mind, feel them in your body, and watch them unfold before your very eyes. You want more money? Feel yourself in the midst of making the most money you want to earn, like you already have it and watch the universe unfold a path for you to obtain it. You want better health? Focus your thoughts on feeling healthy and vibrant, and watch your body change before your very eyes.

Another important factor in supporting this change within yourself is to begin to take note of who you're surrounding yourself with, as you are the sum of the six people you spend the most time with. Are the people around you positive thinkers? Or are they always making fun of other people, and portraying a sense of false self-confidence? Are the people around you positive and always supporting you to change, grow, and inspiring you to do better in your own life?

Indeed, we are the designers of our own life, and this includes our friends and loved ones. We do have the choice as to who we spend time with, and if you're choosing to give your time away to people who are keeping you stagnant, keeping you down and not inspiring you, then you're choosing to remain in a place that is not serving your soul. However, if you make a choice to attract into your life people that are inspiring, people that are accomplishing their true soul's desires, people that are using their time on this earth to then inspire and help others, you'll be lifted up to their resonance, making your transformation more supported, and more abundant. You won't be swimming upstream so to speak, you'll be held and uplifted in a nurturing way.

If you're wondering why an accomplished person who is driven would even want to be your friend, when you yourself think you have nothing to offer, then think of it this way… you're giving another person an opportunity to uplift and inspire another being, and this is the greatest gift you could give another person. Sure it may feel vulnerable, but through the act of helping people, our soul is filled with more fuel than we know what to do with. So, see? This is giving another person the opportunity to inspire, uplift, and help. For this is such a gift. While simultaneously allowing yourself the blessing of being inspired instead of held down, and once you're inspired, you will be unstoppable!

Touching base on the last question I asked you in the beginning of this chapter, is there a public figure, superhero, or person in your life you see as a self-confident, self empowered person that you want to emulate?

Imagine you're in a car and you're about to leave for a road trip. You have all your snacks ready, your water bottle is filled, and our gas tank is full. The only thing that is missing is your road map. You start to look around and feel confused as to what direction to point the car. You know you want to go to a place where you're going to have fun and feel a sense of great happiness, but you don't know how to get there. In a sense, you don't have a road map because you haven't quite pinpointed your destination. If you're a person who wants to improve, and wants to manifest the life you want, but you don't have a road map, or a sense of what that would feel like for you when you got there, take a moment to look outside of yourself to public figures who you want to be like. People that are doing massive amounts of good in this world, and are helping and inspiring millions!

One practice I do once a week to keep my trajectory on track, is to watch the documentary *I Am Not Your Guru*, which is about Tony Robbins. I also watch a seminar that he offers called, "A Date With Destiny." Tony Robbins has helped, inspired, and driven many people to an inner state of success and self-confidence via the work he did on himself, and now he is committed to sharing that insight with the world. My intention for watching this documentary once a week, is so that I can begin to resonate my being with that of Tony's. I see how he helps people, I feel it in my body. I see how he cultivates himself through drive, commitment, compassion, and love. And I feel that in my own body. I see his faith in the higher power guide him through tricky interactions with people, and how his very faith allows something greater to come in and change the lives of millions and millions of people. I feel that in my body.

I resonate. I fill myself up, and after watching that documentary I leave feeling inspired, knowing what my trajectory is and knowing that the resonance I just obtained will get me there. For I am embedding my sub-conscious mind with the feelings that it will take to vibrate this knowing out into the universe. This will then lead me to manifest my goals, and lead me to having the platform to where I myself will commit my life to inspiring, helping, serving, and awakening others. I know this comes with commitment on a daily basis, so I also commit to spending two hours daily on improving myself. I also commit to always watching my thought patterns, and always take at least an hour every day to visualize the woman I am to become, the woman that is going to help change the world. This is how I have honed in on my great inner-power. Allowing outside inspi-rations to come into your life can serve as a great starting place to really evolve yourself past your own self-given limitations, and allow you to enter back into the knowing that you're already an unlimited being.

Take the time to sink into your heart, listen to that inner-voice that is guiding you, and allow that voice to take you into your full potential, which will then bless and inspire all those around you to do the same. It's a beautiful circle of inspiration we can create with all others in this world, if we choose to accept this mission.

CHAPTER TEN:

Bridging Worlds Through Imagination Activation

*"Every failure brings with it the seed of
an equivalent advantage"*

~ Napoleon Hill

What if I were to tell you, that you are already completely equipped with everything you need to be healthy, happy, rich, and of service? That you already have everything inside of you to enter into a state of incredible health and vitality? That you have everything you need to wake up happy and grateful, every single morning? That you can create an abundance of riches so you no longer worry about paying your bills, but instead you're pulled towards helping others step up in their lives, because you have freed yourself from the everyday thoughts of where your next paycheck is coming from?

There is a world you're choosing to live in now, and the sooner you realize it's a world you created, the sooner you'll step into a state of empowerment, and awakening. You did create the life around you, and if you don't like what you see, that's okay! Alchemize that inner feeling. See it as drive, and a challenge which you are more than equipped to overcome, and then step into the life you want to create! It's really that easy. In our current culture, we have been inundated with the external pressure telling us that change is hard, change takes time, change is painful! This is all an external input you can shirk once you make the DECISION to do so! This decision is an act of self empowerment. It is you saying to the world that you're going to go your own way, and create your own path to happiness, abundance, and unconditional love. Because I am here to tell you honestly, if you don't then no one else is going to do it for you. This is your life, your choices, and your outcomes. You may as well put yourself into fifth gear, and charge full-speed ahead!

Our subconscious mind is the vibrational tuning fork that the external world tunes into, and then brings us what we are asking for from our subconscious mind. If you think of this part of your mind as fertile abundant soil, and every thought you have is a seed that is going to land into that soil, then you better make a conscious choice to plant seeds that you want to see grow! The subconscious mind won't care if it's a seed of negativity, or a seed of positivity. Whatever you put there will be accepted, fertilized, then vibrated out into the external world bringing back that very thing you thought in your mind.

This being a universal truth, one must be aware of what they are thinking all day. This is a very important realization, so read this sentence again. Once you train your mind and start to grow the muscle that is the very awareness which you're working on raising, you can start to negate every negative thought with a positive one. So if a negative thought floats into your head, you notice it and immediately counteract it with a positive thought. Even if you're in a bad mood and you're tired and you aren't fully buying this, do it anyway. Commit to doing this for one week straight, and you will watch your entire life change right before your eyes. Committing to this for one week is a small experiment you can try, that will only show you positive results if done with an open heart and an open mind.

Now that we are raising our awareness and watching ourselves create a strong vibration of positivity into our minds, which then seeps into our subconscious, we will begin to see life bring in more positive circumstances for us to play with. To direct this change even further, we then must begin to infuse ourselves with what we want our life to look like and become in the future, and infuse our current thoughts with those visions!

"Do you want to know what you think about most of the time?
Take a look at the results you're getting.
That will tell you exactly what's going on inside."

~ Bob Proctor

The beginning of this formula starts with a specific goal in mind. We can begin to chart the course of our destiny, and we will have access to insight when we leave our charted direction, so definition of purpose is crucial to getting from point A to point B. As an example, let's say that we have been dealing with health challenges. Our body isn't working as we want it to, we have been experiencing an ailment that no doctor or alternative medicine practitioner has been able to help us with. We feel down and out about our circumstances, and also a bit powerless. We start to feel slightly depressed, and everything we see in our lives is now seen through a lens of inner-pain and struggle.

So we start to read this book, and we think, "my goal is to have a completely healthy body, and I will stop at nothing to reach my goal." This is a very worthwhile goal indeed, and one we should all focus on, on a daily basis whether we are in a state of perfect health or not. For focusing on abundant health will give us the courage, drive, and movement to get anywhere we want in this life. If we are drawn into thinking about our ailment or disease, we then implant that we have that ailment into our subconscious mind, which then vibrates out into our body, and the world reflects that back to us. If we choose to focus on abundant health and wellness, we will then be planting that thought into our subconscious mind and our body will then adapt, change, and rediscover itself in abundant health.

There is something I call "black magic" that happens much in the world of medicine, where a patient goes to a doctor not feeling well, and the doctor then gives an exam and begins to explain to the patient their findings. First of all, let's set the stage of knowing that doctors are trained to seek a problem out. They are trained to find "what's wrong," and trained to explain the common plan of action. This is an old paradigm, and one we can choose to not live by anymore if we have the courage to step into our own power. Most times when a patient goes into a doctor's office in a state of less than abundant health, they are already going in with the mindset that the doctor is more knowledgeable and more powerful than themselves. In that sense, whatever the doctor says must be the truth, and their diagnoses must be what follows in terms of the patient's experience. If that is how you are choosing to enter into a doctor's office, then that will be your experience.

If you see that you have all the power to create your own reality, then you can open a new way of hearing a doctor offer their information, choose to accept their findings, or choose to focus on abundant health and allow the outcome to be influenced with the power of your God-given creation. Choose to see what one may call a "problem" as an opportunity for you to implant new waves of thinking into the subconscious, and change the state of your physical health permanently. Will most people think you're crazy or careless for doing this? Maybe. Has this ever worked for people in the past? Most definitely. People have healed themselves in many miraculous ways, and it is still unfolding today.

There was a patient in the late nineties diagnosed with HIV, and this was before many of the new ways of healing that virus had come to light. The doctor told the patient that he would die from this disease. The patient, not accepting the diagnosis, spent the next year watching funny movies and focusing his mind on laughter, happiness, and abundant health. He chose to never entertain the fact of what the doctor found. One year to the day, he went back and was retested, and was no longer diagnosed with HIV, and he has been in a state of abundant health ever since.

When I say a doctor can use "black magic" this is only if the patient chooses to accept it. If you go to a doctor, and the doctor says, "you have cancer, and you only have three months to live at best," this is a form of black magic that can be then planted into the patient's conscious mind IF the patient believes the doctor. Then the subconscious will accept this seed, and grow the plant that reflects that thought. However, if the patient CHOOSES to not believe the doctor, but to then put forth all the effort he has to BELIEVING, with feeling, that he is perfectly healthy, perfectly abundant in the power to create his own destiny, then his subconscious has no choice but to do whatever is planted inside of it. The body will absorb this new seed, and that vibration can literally change the state of the physical body. This is why training the mind to think only positive thoughts, training the mind to watch the thoughts that pass through it, and training the self to keep this effort up on a daily basis with persistence, is crucial to every being on this planet.

Commit today to taking your power back, to knowing that you in fact do, and can, create your own destiny, and that you're more powerful than you know. Set a goal of repetition in affirmations, or reading and re-reading this book until it has planted this as a knowing in your life, then choose to take your power back from the external circumstances that the OLD you created. Be persistent and committed in creating the new you in the new life you truly desire to live.

I myself went through this teaching, and came out on the other end of it, now knowing without a fraction of a doubt that I do change the health of my body with my mind, and I do create everything in my own life. There was a time when I began to get sick, really sick. I got shingles, and once my shingles healed I got a cold, then a flu. Then another cold, and so on for four months straight. I was not in my vitality, and I was in a state of helplessness. I was seeking the counsel of doctors, and began to try to figure out what was happening to my body. I was taking this supplement, and that supplement, all with the prayer that I wouldn't be sick anymore. I was focusing on how sick I was, and how bad I wanted to get better. I was planting the seed of sickness in my mind, and that is how I was feeling.

I began to get tested for internal levels of toxicity, thinking maybe my immune system was suppressed. The test results indeed came back positive with high levels of toxins, and my doctor recommended a detox regime that was quite intensive, and lasted three months. Running for thirty minutes, daily followed by two hours of sweating in a sauna, while take a regime of supplements to help my body detox. On top of this, I was telling my friends and family the story the doctor had told me, and I was feeding that ailment that I had too many toxins in my body, and that is why I was sick. I was creating that as my accepted reality.

As I was following the prescribed detox regime, I was focusing on getting the toxins out of my body. So guess what? The toxins remained in my body! I was focusing on my body being toxic, and therefore I had toxins! It's really that simple! I shortly realized that I was creating a self-perpetuating loop of health. Focusing on toxins creates toxins, and focusing on health and vitality creates health and vitality! I got re-tested a month in, and found out that yes indeed, toxins were still in my body, and yes indeed, more toxins had arrived!

This is when I had the realization, that all the philosophies I was implementing in my own life for creating my own destiny and abundance, was also completely applicable to my health, and I was going about changing the state of my health in a backwards fashion, when now I knew that I knew better! I decided to take my power back, to create the health I wanted out of my body with my thoughts, and I set a goal. I was going to take the next two months, to focus on a state of pure health and vitality, to take care of my body by eating beautiful organic foods, to run and enjoy movement, to love myself with self-care and exercise. To only know myself as a healthy young, beautiful woman, and to enter into that knowing with every cell of my body. I committed to those two months, and then went back to the doctor to get re-tested, not telling the doctor that I dropped the regime of having to sweat the toxins out on a daily basis with a sauna, but that I used my mind to change the state of health in my body by KNOWING. And planting that KNOWING in my subconscious, that my body was already perfectly healthy and abundant. What do you suppose the difference was in the test when I went back two months later? YES, IT WAS PERFECT HEALTH! I no longer had high-toxin levels in my system, and I was not surprised. As I focused on health, I got healthy. And when I focused on toxins I got toxins! The simplicity of this way of living is quite incredible and powerful!

If we are sick, or poor, or in a bad relationship and we want to create a different life for ourselves, how do we bridge that gap when everything in front of us says something other than what we want? How do we overcome the sense of defeat that seems to look us in the eye? We IMAGINE a different life. We make believe until the make believe is a reality. You were given the gift of imagination as a kid, and that gift is still quite alive inside of you now, just waiting to be fed again. So feed it!

Every day, wake up and imagine yourself in a bed that is meant for royalty! Imagine your health in a perfect state of vitality. Imagine millions of dollars resting in your bank account, and imagine it like you already own it and have it in your current possession! Imagination is one of the master skeleton keys to getting whatever it is you want of this life, and it's an incredible design tool for that masterpiece you'll be proud to call your life!

If you have a hard time imagining, then make it a point to spend time with a child once a week, and have them show you how completely easy it is to make believe. To pretend you're a princess, or king or queen, and what that life feels like, and looks like. Make it a point to play more and laugh more, and see the little things that are beautiful in your life, to alchemize your current inner mindset from one of negativity to positivity.

I spend AT LEAST two hours every day imagining myself in the life I want to create for myself. I see myself holding hands with my husband and walking through nature with him. I see and feel him kissing me and holding me, and taking me out to dinner. I see him opening the car door for me, and helping me in my life become the best me possible. I see the level of my savings account grow and grow further on a daily basis, and I see the people that I can reach and help to inspire, grow to millions. I see myself traveling the world and teaching seminars, inspiring millions of people to create the life they want to live. I see all the happy faces smiling back at me as my career blossoms. I see myself surrounded by the most influential people in this world as we team up to lift society into new heights. I do this all with feeling on a daily basis, and I never fail to complete this state of make believe, ever. It happens every day, and it is persistence and drive that feed my desire. This is the fuel that is going to propel my life to unfold just how I want it to unfold. Not because I wished it, but because I desire it. And I know I can make anything happen.

I know without a fraction of a doubt that if I put consistent energy into something, that I follow the steps the universe lays out before me which have been created by my subconscious mind, that I then cannot fail, ever. Many people will say, "well I tried this, and it didn't work." I say to them, "are you still practicing? Or have you given up?" Because true success will be met with many, many instances to test your persistence and desires. If you give up at the first, second, or even third sign of defeat, then the universe will deem you not worthy and you will be met with the same fate as most of the population, deeming this philosophy as one that doesn't work. In truth, you MUST have persistence, and your desire to fulfill the goal you are reaching towards must be so strong in every cell of your body that if met with a road block, you see that very road block as another challenge from the universe to test the strength of desire. Then your drive takes over once again, and you find another way to overcome every obstacle put before you. As Napoleon Hill states, "every failure brings with it the seed of an equivalent advantage." This is one of the most empowering, beautiful sentiments I have chosen to live by. For this statement fills me with the very knowing that nothing can stop me but myself. Did you know that Thomas Edison went through 10,000 different experiments before he got the light bulb to work? He said, "I haven't failed, I just found 10,000 ways that don't work."

What is it that you long to acquire? What health would you like to manifest for yourself? In what ways are your current modes of thinking feeding the current state you're in rather than lifting you into the knowing that you have the power to create the reality you so desire? Do you have someone in your life that can currently support you in obtaining this goal?

During this process of re-creating ourselves, it is most crucial that we have an accountability partner who can keep us on track. A partner that will not talk down to us, or call us crazy for reaching for something most don't have the courage to reach for. Choose someone that can hear your goals, agree to support you in obtaining them, and always stay as your behind-the-scenes cheerleader, for this will help you exponentially. There are life coaches all around you, skillfully trained to support people like you that are hungry for change. Hungry for a better life, and are willing to go the extra mile to support you in reaching whatever it is you set your mind to. There will be a list of resources in the back of this book to help you get to that end goal, and I encourage you to invest in yourself now, for if you don't know, no one else will.

Work on yourself and the rest will come. If you see a life coach's fee structure, and you think you can't afford it, then you won't be able to afford it. If you see a coach's fee structure with the mindset that no matter what, you will utilize all the help you can get to reach that end goal of abundance, then you'll make the payment happen. And you'll see great results unfold for yourself in this life, and perhaps even become a life coach yourself one day!

Reward is another important reminder. For as you begin to change, focus on what IS changing, and reward yourself. This is a mindset of positivity. If you change in many ways, and you choose to focus on the couple of other attributes that you have yet to evolve out of, this would be an example of a negative mindset, and you must choose to propagate a positive mindset to create growth and expansion. Negativity breeds more negativity, and contracts the body, while positivity opens the body and creates nothing but positivity.

Your imagination is your bridge from your current state into the state you wish to manifest. See it, feel it, and believe it like it is already taking place in your life now. As you drive to work, see yourself already living this new life. As you eat your lunch, see yourself eating with that partner you wish to manifest. As you jog for the day, see your body stronger than a Greek God! As you begin to flex the imagination muscle, it WILL grow, it will get stronger, and it will begin to plant into your subconscious mind all that you wish to obtain into this life. All you have to do is make a definite decision to do this with persistence, desire, and never give up! See every failure as a challenge that you have no qualms overcoming, and see each obstacle as a growth opportunity that is going to sculpt you in beautiful ways you have yet to even imagine. Make this mindset your everyday reality, and watch the magical powers you were given at birth unfold before your very eyes....

> *"When you have exhausted all possibilities,*
> *remember this: You haven't."*
>
> ~ Thomas Edison

Acknowledgements

I have been blessed with many people surrounding me who confirm either knowingly or unknowingly the path I am on, and assisted me in completing my overall goal of helping millions of people. I would like to start by thanking my parents, for both of them have been a complete inspiration and source of growth for me since birth. I was taught faith, magic, and the known fact that I am limitless, by my mother, who always saw me as the woman I am now becoming. She never ever once gave up knowing that I would be not just a shooting star for this planet to admire, but a meteor that would one day change the world we live in. For this, mom, I am filled to the brim with gratitude. I honor the woman you made yourself into, for it was through watching you overcome your own obstacles in life, that made me know I could overcome any challenge I was ever faced with, and so I did. My father, who taught me strength, persistence, and the beauty of being a success in business. Your undying love and affection for me awakened me to the powerful woman I am now, and you too held onto this vision of my greatness when I felt nothing of the sort in regards to myself. You held this vision for me until I stepped into it and honored it myself, and your very perseverance through my troubled era was an astounding accomplishment. I love you both more than words can speak.

To my brother, who became my rock. You held me up and spoke to me clearly when I would spin out into nothingness, and you always confirmed my job well done. Your subtle ways of supporting me kept me balanced even when you weren't looking, and you taught me how to keep my mind balanced and to always see the good in people, for you always saw the good in me. To my sister, who kept a beautiful ability of staying positive through all the trials life threw at you, and you stayed on top even when the top was a huge hill to climb. You raised three beautiful, incredible daughters with so much style and grace, that you have become a beautiful mother of inspiration for me when I have my own children.

To my cousin Adam, you have been a silent sense of support, always loving me and thinking I was special. You introduced me and sponsored me to learn transcendental meditation, and this practice has changed my life! I no longer live in the hamster wheel of stress, now I am the entire universe that supports the very energy that I harness.

To Esalen Institute, a place where I went when nothing else served me, and created a platform for me to love myself again. To all the teachers and facilitators who hold space for those who earnestly want to change, and who take their lives back one tear at a time. To Jo Cavanaugh, who knew I was hiding from my life and took the time, energy, and effort to wake me up out of my painful slumber. This was the most beautiful offering anyone could have given me, for it awoke me to myself, and I have been on the fast track to filling out my sense of knowing ever since.

To David and Marcia Radin, you both created the most beautiful retreat space I have ever known. It is so incredible and special. Your teachings filled me with awareness and a sense of respect for myself that I had yet to feel, and this respect was the birth of a new version of myself that allowed me to hold the flame for others to awaken. I will always honor, love, and devote my heart to what you gave me. To Diane, for introducing me to yoga, and all the love and devotion you gave me and the rest of the students. It was an incredible thing to watch such a powerful woman stand in her power, and you inspired me to do the same.

To Joseph Goldstein, I thank you for creating IMS and introducing me to Vippassana Meditation. The retreats that transpire on your land, truly do create a quiet in my heart that then allows me to hear and see what is really going on around me. The silence lead to a truth, and this truth lead to an awakening on deeper levels. I am so grateful for the space you hold for others to be in silence, for I feel silence is the most important thing we can rest in now, when the world has become so busy and so loud.

To Dan and Sue Rututa, your creation of Crestone healing Arts School was the most beautiful soul warrior training I ever got to participate in. It showed me my inner strength, pushed me to break wide open, and then you held me as another more stronger, healthier version of myself emerged. This strength and perseverance will always stay with me, as I walk this planet and honor this planet. For it is you who taught me that every step I take is a kiss for the earth and a bow to the sun, and this honoring charges me back up on a daily basis. The space you hold changes the world and creates spiritual warriors, and this is indeed changing the planet.

To Bob Proctor and Sandy Gallagher, the teachings you transmute to your students are indeed very applicable, and very real for everything you say is wisdom from the universe. This wisdom was the key that unlocked the door to my productive soul, and allowed me to then apply all of my past wisdom into life form so I can share myself with the world on a daily basis, completing my goal of changing this planet into one where love, respect, and abundance is created for everyone on the planet. The daily rituals you inspired me to perform, are the current backbone of my life, and this backbone holds me strong and true to my authenticity.

To Tony Robbins, your strength and ability to cultivate yourself into the man you are today showed me that I too was on the same track as you, and we are indeed kindred spirits. I resonated with you through your teachings and felt for the first time in my life, everything I had done up until that point was not strange and not out of whack, but in line with greatness and change. For to make a new world, we must step out of the current world we know. Your very act of doing this, confirmed my knowing that I too was here to change this world, and I too can cultivate the strength and self-confidence to be myself no matter what, all the time. The wisdom you share, seeps into the cracks of my soul, and awakens me to the possibility that is ever expanding and growing right before my very eyes. I felt alone in my mission until I met you and your teachings, and this resonance is my jet fuel pack. I bow in gratitude towards your efforts.

Cristo and Oscar, you two have truly changed the lives of many, many magical horses, and for this I will always bow in gratitude. Doma India, of Argentina is a method that opened me up to the beauty that is all around me. It taught me how to listen to the energy behind the words and succeeded in connected me into a circle of trust with my horse. My future is going to shine brighter because of your energy, presence, and love that you share with the world. Thank you.

To Tessa and Amy, you girls saw my bright light and never stopped seeing it. You held me in a way I have never been held before with girl friends. You loved me unconditionally, and saw me as exceptional, and this vision allowed myself to believe it. To Scott, you're the first man I have been able to trust fully with every cell of my body, and you continue to love and support me through every trial and tribulation I encounter. You see me as the brightest light this world has ever seen. This brings tears to my eyes. You loved me even though we went to hell and back, and for this devotion, I will always be there for you no matter what.

To Peggy McColl, for creating the most brilliant book writing program to date. For your combination of self-study along with the productivity that suits today's rapid pace, tuned me into accomplishing this very book you read. Peggy awoke the giant in my heart, and gave a practical path for that giant to then express itself, making me feel accomplished, exposed, and of service to this world. I will forever be grateful for the woman you created inside of yourself, and for your devotion to me and everyone else in your courses. You are incredible.

To Joseph Cavanaugh, you have been such a pillar for me in this life, and I can't help but think we have helped one another in many previous lives as well. You stood by me as I wrote this book, then took the time and energy to give me exceptional feedback that then allowed this book to become the beautiful work of art that it is. Thank you for giving your life to helping all those around you. Without you I am not sure where I would have landed 15 years ago.

To all the other beautiful souls I have not mentioned by name, but who carry themselves through this world with integrity, devotion to others, and devotion to evolving themselves to help this world shift and awaken all those on the planet. I love you.

Resources

AWARENESS RAISING RETREATS

Esalen Institute
Big Sur, CA.
www.esalen.org

Body Mind Restoration Retreats
Ithaca, New York
www.bodymindretreats.com

Insight Meditation Society
Barre, MA
www.Dharma.org

Eponaquest
Amado, AZ
Eponaquest.com

Scarpati Doma India
San Luis, Argentina
www.domaindiascarpati.com

SELF DEVELOPMENT SEMINARS

Tony Robbins
www.tonyrobbins.com

Bob Proctor and Sandy Gallagher
www.proctorgallagherinstitute.com

Peggy McColl
www.Peggymccoll.com

Matrix Energetics
www.matrixenergetics.com

SUCCESS COACH

Tessa Manning
www.infinitelysuccessful.com

EVOLUTIONARY BODY WORK

Mo Washburn
www.mowashburn.com

BOOKS

The Book of Joy
By: the Dalai Lama and Desmond Tutu

Think and Grow Rich
By: Napoleon Hill (and any other book by Napoleon Hill)

Awaken the Giant Within
By: Tony Robbins (and any other book by Tony Robbins)

You were Born Rich
By: Bob Proctor (and any other book by Bob Proctor)

Your Destiny Switch
By: Peggy McColl

The Power of your subconscious Mind
By: Joseph Murphy

Steve Jobs
By: Walter Isaacson

Transcendental Meditation
By: Jack Forem

The Experience of Insight
By: Joseph Goldstein

Loving Kindness, the Revolutionary art of Happiness
By: Sharon Salzberg

The Tao of Equus
By: Linda Kohanov

Lifting the Veil
By: Joseph Michael Levry

The Hidden Power
By: Thomas Troward

About the Author

Seraphim Fire Photography

Scarlet Ravin is best known for her unique ability to see through people to their core, enabling her to bring about profound change and daily inspiration to the lives of her clients. Her way of seeing the world is indeed bringing a new world into being, through her daily work with clients all over the globe, sharing new perspectives on how they can adopt a new way of being. The readings she channels help to open new pathways for her clients, releasing old patterns and allowing one to fully show up in abundance in the present moment.

Scarlet has been traveling around the world and studying from many different teachers since 2001, and is now compiling that found information into this very book for the masses to read. Her intention has always been to understand herself, and through that understanding be able to bring about change for other people.

Her profound dedication to helping others truly understand their own greatness is her core driving fuel, and she will stop at nothing to help the people of this world awaken to their full potential.

She is an entrepreneur and understands the path to a successful business, having created three successful companies herself. Her ability to transform the spiritual teachings into practical daily application has helped thousands transform their lives. She enjoys spending time with her horse, running through the desert and sharing intimate time with her close friends and family. To learn more about Scarlet go to **www.scarletravin.com**.

Testimonials from Scarlet's Sessions

"*I have been on an amazing journey since our last session. Intense, Rich, and Transformational. Considering safety and self image have unlocked a lot of old stuff. At one point last Saturday I felt like I was being cleansed via suction in a swirling way from my tail bone. This was after sensing an energy leak in my field and self-treating. I've gained much clarity into the symptom of compulsive eating, drinking, smoking, shopping. Seeking safety and being fully known and loved in that full knowing. It's like a convergence of the clues coming in for years – since I got sober I sense. And last night, I was really me at a small dinner and I enjoyed myself so much – easily setting aside the intense self reflection for some light hearted pleasure.*"
– T.Y., Psychologist

"*A friend of mine purchased a Matrix Energetics session for me with Scarlet because she knew that 1. I really needed it and 2. a part of me tends to be avoidant and wary of things I can't explain. I am so glad that she did! During the session, I felt deeply seen and known on a soul level. Although I have never met Scarlet in person, she identified, named and worked on patterns and truths that brought me to tears, to many moments of deep recognition of truth, clarity of purpose and to an easing of heavy, dark, felt-sense sensations within me. I felt warm, light and cleansed at the end of our session. In the following weeks, an unbelievable series of synchronistic events revealed the degree to which I was surrounded by lies, deception, illusion and harmful people in my life. Although the truths were painful, it felt like Light and Truth swept through my life and did some major housecleaning, and that I had the inner resources to weather the storm. The healing session I had with Scarlet played a significant and integral role in the shift I was needing to make on a soul level. I am deeply grateful for it and highly recommend it.*"
– Yvette, E., Psychologist

"*My session with Scarlet came at a time in my life when I felt heavy and alone. Most things in my life were being converted into proof that I did not have any meaningful purpose and I was not feeling connected in most of my relationships. For 5 years now I have been practicing Zen meditation, implemented a non-inflammatory diet, have had many Cranial sacral sessions and am continuing to learn about new modes of healing. All of these healing practices have greatly benefited my life and have decreased suffering caused by Juvenile Rheumatoid Arthritis and progressive vision loss.*

The Matrix Energetics sessions I have had with Scarlet have given me insight into core instances of trauma that have been causes of great suffering. The awareness and gentle release of some of these experiences have benefited me physically and mentally. As a Matrix Energetics practitioner Scarlet is mindful, open-hearted, and most importantly, light and playful. It was easy to talk to her and she took the time to thoroughly explain the practice before we began and she continually checks in with me. For those of us that have a feeling or idea that we hold all the information and wisdom within ourselves to make the changes that will allow us to radiate a brighter Light, I recommend having a conversation with Scarlet! Much love to you all."

– Alejandro Urias, Teacher

"You have helped me and some of my good friends so much. I've stopped smoking for good this year, I'm done with it and not in a bad way. I'm so glad I smoked and so glad I stopped. I've heard so many good things from the people I referred to you and I know you are a gifted healer. I will be calling soon to get some more work started, but for now I feel great, have a love in my life and am getting so much healthier."

– Mark T., Psychologist

"I still don't know how it happened, or how she did it. I live in Oregon, and Scarlet lives in northern California, and she looked inside of my body as though I was on an operating table. She prepared me by asking me some questions about any issue or issues that I would like to work on in my life. This was done on the phone, and she said she would call right back. My grand niece(who is 27) was visiting me at the time and Scarlet offered to do a session for her as well. She asked Sarah the same questions, saying she would call us both back.

Scarlet had said that we might feel something. So Sarah and I were sitting on two different couches trying to figure out what that meant. We started chatting and we started laughing, and we couldn't stop either. I haven't laughed that much in a long, long time. So we tried to get it together, and get serious. I told Sarah, as she was going to get a session first, to lay down and try to relax. She lay down and started to relax, and said oooohh... she was feeling waves of energy in her mid section.

I too had a similar experience. I won't go into the details, but suffice to say, Scarlet told the both of us things about our lives that only we knew.

I would like Scarlet to explain the laughter to all of you, it was wonderful. She is truly gifted"

– Linda T., Artist

"I had the honor to meet and work with Scarlet at a sacred retreat center in Ithaca, NY. Each one of us in this world is inherently designed to thrive and shine in our own unique way. Scarlet shines in serving other beings; whether it be preparing a meal full of love and intention, guiding words into asana, cleaning a toilet or channeling spirit.

My most poignant experience with Scarlet's healing touch was after an incident of accidentally stabbing my left palm with the blade of a food processor. The blade punctured my palm deeply leaving a gapping hole. The doctors on sight said I needed stitches; I opted for zinc oxide, healing thoughts and not using my hand for some time. The wound healed nicely but pain continued to persist. Scarlet asked if she could help. As we sat together my hand held by hers, some time passed and then I literally felt the trauma in my palm being pulled out. Visually I suppose I can describe it as noodle being pulled from soup. The pain was not only mitigated but completely absent. I've much gratitude to know and have such a healer/friend in my life."

– Michael Graves, CMT/Healer

"I had the pleasure of performing live music during a yoga class taught by Scarlet, and it was a very deep experience for all present. Wonderful, warm hearted teacher!"

– Billy White, Musician

"Dear Scarlet,

As you know I have been dealing with cancer for a number of years. During my healing process I was fortunate enough to receive reiki treatment from you at Esalen. I want you to know that the reiki treatment that you gave me was an important component of my healing process. The healing energy that was transferred into my body during the treatment that you gave to me enabled my body to have the strength to continue with my treatment and rid myself of this disease. I now have no more symptoms of my cancer. Thank you for your part in my healing process."

– John Fitton, Psychologist

"Scarlet sees what the eyes can't see and hears what the ears don't hear. She held me in the most sacred manner while working on my heart during a Reiki session. She is a skilled and compassionate healer. Be prepared for deep conversations filled with love and light."

– Chris Holder, Naturopathic Doctor

If you're interested in booking a session with Scarlet
please email **scarlet@scarletravin.com** and
visit **www.scarletravin.com** for more information.

WHITE FOX
MEDICINALS

Healing With Cannabis,
The Alchemy of White Fox Medicinals™

*"White Fox Medicinals™ is the new wave of medicine coming through to
shift this world into a new state of awareness.
We do control our health to a certain extent, and this alchemical offering
helps us achieve what our heart truly desires."*

~ SCARLET RAVIN

I spent the greater part of my childhood and early adulthood going to hospitals and doctor's offices to be told, "here just take this pill," in regards to the pain or discomfort I was feeling. It didn't matter if it was from a sore throat, or a stomachache, or painful growing pains. Every Western doctor I encountered had the same conclusion, "here take this pill." I didn't know any better at the time, but after years of studying holistic health practices, and how the mind affects the body's health, I now see a beautiful gap of opportunity in Western health practices. Truth be told, we cannot just treat the body, for we are not one-dimensional creatures. We are multi-dimensional creatures, and if we just treat the symptoms we are selling ourselves short.

I came into contact with cannabis at a young age, however I didn't realize the medicinal benefits until I came into adulthood, and began to test different strains in regards to specific intentions I wanted to heal, in regards to my health. I would test this strain for back pain, and that strain for muscle pain and this strain for headaches... etc. I found something amazing – there are specific strains that can magically open the pathways of our brain, and change how we relate to what it is we are working on healing in the first place. It's not the pain we must focus on healing, or the disease. It's the pattern we have chosen to consciously think about, in regards to how we see our pain or disease. Once we shift that inner mental vision, we can permanently change our entire health. This is alchemy, the transmutation of one element into another with magic... our thoughts are the magic.

It's true, not all strains are created equal, so I spent the better part of two years testing the phenotypes of over 26 strains I started from seed, and smoked each one separately to see it's brain pathway benefits. I felt a little close to defeat when I found her...Northern Lights! She was the first strain that lifted my old thought patterns, and then showed me new ways of seeing the issue, allowing more opportunity to come through and then shift my actual physical circumstance. It felt like a miracle to me, and this discovery inspired me to create "White Fox Medicinals™" working with my coveted Northern Lights strain to be the cornerstone of my medicine.

I began to listen to deep inner-guidance as I formulated each tincture, for each specific category of issues people seem to be having difficulty resolving. My goal was to provide an alternative medicine that people could consume on a daily basis, that would not just heal the physical body and it's symptoms, but the mental thought patterns that keep the physical issue stuck. I also wanted to create formulations that would allow people to consume daily, without losing their ability to drive, to work, or to function at their highest capacity. After a year of formulations, I came up with the perfect level of THC/CBD combinations, while utilizing alchemical traditions to incorporate other herbs, to also assist the cannabis in grounding the health shift into the physical body.

I found that when I took cannabis alone, I was working on more of a higher dimensional level, and it almost felt like my body was a bit left out. When I incorporated other healing herbs, I realized the healing not only occurred mentally and emotionally, but also physically. It grounded the shift into my body. A miracle was born!

I chose to label each medicinal tincture with an animal totem, as when one is relating to a symptom they are trying to shift, there can be a rigidity in that relating. Meaning, when you think of relieving yourself of anxiety, and you think the word "anxiety," your body has a tendency to feel the energy of how you relate to that word for strengthening the pattern. If we relate to our anxiety with the soothing thought of a whale swimming through the deep blue ocean, a soothing mellow vibration enters our body and we no longer feel the tension of anxiety, but we feel the release of the thought of a whale swimming in the ocean.

When you look around the website **www.whitefoxmedicinals.com** and see the animal totems, your body will feel the imprint of this totem and relax or strengthen your resolve, depending on the totem. In this sense, we can bypass the strengthening of what we want to shift, and begin to train our mind to focusing on what we want to feed. Every totem I chose, carries a specific message in direct relation to the symptoms that are alchemically designed to be shifted in your system, when consumed in a healthy protocol. The totem will guide you to higher spiritual realms, the CBD/THC medicine may shift the pathways in the brain and may shift the cellular structure of the body, while the herbs may ground all this change in the physical.

Enjoy the journey, and see everything happening to your health as an opportunity for the growth of your soul. If you choose to see your life in this way you'll be unstoppable! I have also written a book getting into more detail of this medicine, and how one can see and shift their thought patterns in regards to health and healing. I also provide you with an educational worksheet in regards to the different aspects of intentional healing for yourself. Explore your health like you explore the website of White Fox Medicinals™, with the wide eyes of a child and the curiosity of a puppy. May the force be with you!

Scarlet Ravin
International bestselling author

"*Each session with Scarlet brings awareness to emerging aspects of myself. Supported by her insight and genuine care, I carry forward a sense of empowerment to embrace the life I want to create*".
– **Karen Kopacz, Brand Strategist & Designer**

"*I love the pain salve and massage oil, I instantly felt more calm and my pain felt relieved. I love the use of animal totems in the product line, and all the tinctures are very potent and taste amazing. These medicinals are helping me heal and feel more at peace.*"
– **Cami Walker, *New York Times* Best Selling Author *29 Gifts: How a Month of Giving can change your life* and creator of www.29gifts.org**

"*I can't say enough good things about this line, specifically the 'owl pain salve' product for my sore muscles. I apply it every night, and it helps to relax my sore and tight muscles and sleep deeply. I am very sensitive to the energetic of products, and this one had an immediate resonance for me. Incredible impressed, as I haven't found anything that works this well for me or my husband before, ever!*"
– **J.R., Naturopathic Doctor**

"In the line of what I do, which is lots of lifting and moving heavy pots of bone broth, my body especially my arms and shoulders are really sore at the end of the day. I noticed that from the day I put your Owl Salve on these parts of my body I could feel the soreness in the muscle dissipate. It smells like nothing I've ever tried (This is a good thing) before and I love it because it doesn't leave you with an oily skin and the smell vanishes rather quickly once exposed to air."

– Cesar Vernier, Chef

"I was using all the products in my vast natural healing toolbox to help control the pain and speed the healing of 3 fractured ribs, all without much success. I started using the Owl Salve and felt an almost immediate shift into pain relief. I am so grateful to have found a product so well crafted with healing intention! It is my new go-to in my bag of natural healing tricks."

– Marta Claire Du-Lacey, Clar Senses Body Work

"I clumsily cut into the edge of my big toe nail fold and lacerated it to the flesh which made my toe bleed for a while. When I went to put my socks and shoes on to go to work the next day, my toe was throbbing immensely. I am on my feet all day every day so this was a big problem for me. When I would come home from work my sock would be covered in blood. I tried Neosporin and arnica and even took ibuprofin but nothing gave my toe any relief. A few days after the incident I ran into Scarlet at the horse barn and told her about what had happened. She told me about the Owl Pain Away Salve she had just made and gave me a sample to try. I took the salve home that night and applied it right away. The pain dulled almost immediately! After days of agony I finally found relief! I started to apply the salve in the morning and again in the afternoon. The laceration healed within two weeks and thanks to the Owl Pain Away salve I was able to work without being bothered by pain! I recommend it to anyone with aches, pains, sores and wounds!"

– Tatjana Kovac, Vet Tech

"I'd previously thought of CBD oil as something to use for pain relief and was using White Fox's Horse CBD oil to help with acute bodily pain after a fall. What I'd unexpectedly received along with the pain relief was the return of a solid night's sleep! I'd tried other natural remedies to help with the effects of Menopause and an increase in anxiety due to lack of sleep. I am so very happy to have found this natural and nurturing CBD oil to erase my nighttime anxiety and insomnia."

– O.S. ESQ

"I feel cared for when I use White Fox Medicinal™ products. The care put into each step of it's creation is palpable. From the gorgeous Miron glass containers, to the absolutely divine smell of the Owl Salve and White Crow massage oils, to the healing story and animal totem imagery given with each product to help guide myself through the healing process – each product commands my attention! When I have these products around I am delight-fully compelled to take conscious time for myself. Using the oils and salves is, for me, the equivalent of taking an any day moment and shifting it into a sacred time for my well being."
– P.J.C, ND

Scarlet Ravin
International bestselling author

www.whitefoxmedicinals.com
scarlet@whitefoxmedicinals.com

Scarlet Ravin
has two more books releasing in 2017.

"Healing with Cannabis, the Alchemy of White Fox Medicinals™"

A masterpiece in itself, for people seeking to gain information on cannabis as a medicine, the understanding behind cannabis culture and what to do with ingesting cannabis on a regular basis to heal, soothe and transform your being. Education is empowerment, and this book will lay the insightful foundation for anyone seeking to incorporate cannabis into their daily health regimen, with the knowledge and insight to allow the medicine to heal in the most intentional way possible. Get to know your healing path better, and enhance the insight you have already obtained with this incredible and insightful book.

This book is also the precursor to the online classes offered by Scarlet through her website **www.whitefoxmedicinals.com** where everyone will have access to a cannabis health guide, learning how to enhance their healing and utilize the medicine intentionally. New research is always being released, so visit the White Fox Medicinals™ website to stay up to date on the latest information on how cannabis can lead to healing.

"Scarlet's Little Book of Secrets"

This is one of those small but powerful books offered by Scarlet, opening her heart and stepping into vulnerability, as she shares some of her life moments that offered a pivotal amount of insight. It was through her toughest times that she became the most strong, the most insightful. The intention of this book of secrets is to offer a look inside one's spiritual journey, to find that at the end of the day, we are all human, we are all connected, and we are all in this together. The strength we can obtain from being vulnerable is perhaps the most profound, for it can also inspire those around us to show their true selves, and when one steps into this power in their own life, they are unstoppable.

The Literary Fairies

we make your literary wish come true

Scarlet Ravin

has partnered with

The Literary Fairies

who have a mission to give to those who have
experienced an adversity or disability an opportunity
to become a published author while sharing
a story to uplift, inspire and entertain the world.

Visit TLF website to find out how YOU
could become a published author or where
you can help grant a literary wish.

More details provided at
www.theliteraryfairies.com

Printed in Great Britain
by Amazon